Key Stage 3
Teachers' Guide

EDUCATIONAL

Mathematics

Alan Smith

Every effort has been made to trace copyright holders and to obtain their permission for the use of copyright material. The authors and publishers will gladly receive information enabling them to rectify any error or omission in subsequent editions.

First published 1998

Letts Educational
Schools and Colleges Division
9–15 Aldine Street
London W12 8AW
Tel 0181 740 2270
Fax 0181 740 2280

Text: © Alan Smith 1998

Design and illustrations © BPP (Letts Educational) Ltd 1998

Design and page layout: Ken Vail Graphic Design, Cambridge

Illustrations: Ken Vail Graphic Design

All our rights reserved. No part of this publication may be reproduced, stored in a retrieval system, or transmitted, in any form or by any means, electronic, mechanical, photocopying, recording or otherwise, without prior permission of Letts Educational.

British Library Cataloguing-in-Publication Data

A CIP record for this book is available from the British Library
ISBN 1 84085 130 9

Printed and Bound in Great Britain by Ashford Colour Press

Letts Educational is the trading name of
BPP (Letts Educational) Ltd

Contents

Introduction

Level 4

1	Place value and powers of 10	1
2	Numbers and number patterns	3
3	Fractions and percentages	5
4	Working with decimals	6
5	Coordinates	7
6	2-D shapes and 3-D models	9
7	Units and scales	11
8	Perimeter, area and volume	13
9	Looking at data	15
10	Introducing probability	18
	Review	19

Level 5

11	Decimals and negative numbers	20
12	Multiplication and division without a calculator	22
13	Fractions and percentages	23
14	Rounding and estimation	25
15	Algebra	27
16	Geometry of 2-D shapes	29
17	Metric and imperial measures	32
18	Averages and frequency diagrams	33
19	Charts and line graphs	37
20	Theoretical and experimental probability	41
	Review	43

Level 6

21	Rounding and approximation	45
22	Number patterns	47
23	Fractions, decimals and percentages	49
24	Linear equations	51
25	Functions and graphs	53
26	Quadrilaterals and angles	60
27	Making shapes using *Logo*	62
28	Area and volume	65
29	The circle: area and circumference	66
30	Enlargement and reflection	68
31	Frequency diagrams and pie charts	75
32	Scatter diagrams and other graphs	79
33	Probability	84
	Review	86

Teachers' Guide (with answers)
Introduction

This book contains answers to all of the exercises and reviews in the Letts KS3 classbook. There are also brief notes for teachers attached to each exercise.

Most of the answers given are exact, although some of the results to numerical calculations have been rounded (e.g. area of a circle), and therefore other variations are perfectly acceptable. Similarly some of the answers are only approximate because they have been measured from a diagram or graph; this is usually indicated where appropriate.

Answers to certain key questions are given in the back of the classbook; these answers are also included within the full answers in this book.

The notes that accompany each section are designed to amplify the key point behind a particular exercise, or to anticipate difficulties with any particular question. While much of their content will be obvious to a trained and experienced teacher, it is hoped that these brief notes will be especially helpful to the non-specialist or newly-qualified mathematics teacher.

Level 4 Unit 1
Place value and powers of 10

Throughout this chapter, watch for bad habits creeping into written work. Commonly seen are:
wrong use of commas, e.g. 53,600 instead of 53 600;
columns in additions/subtractions not set up correctly.

Exercise 1.1

Section 1.1 may be introduced using examples on the board such as 'Explain the meaning of the 8 in each of these numbers: 1084, 328, 168 472' and so on. The problems in Exercise 1.1 are restricted to hundred-thousands or less; more adventurous pupils might need some harder questions involving millions etc.

1 4266
2 13 593
3 11 405
4 20 907
5 33 108
6 9080
7 5049
8 13 200
9 20 003
10 700 056
11 Six thousand, three hundred and ninety-four
12 Seven thousand and thirty-two
13 Twelve thousand, three hundred and forty-two
14 Sixty-three thousand, two hundred and seven
15 Ninety thousand, two hundred and sixty-five
16 Fourteen thousand, two hundred and five
17 Seven thousand and seventy-three
18 Ten thousand and five
19 Sixty-seven thousand, two hundred and fifty-six
20 Thirty-two thousand and sixty-seven

Exercise 1.2

Section 1.2 should be very familiar to all, from primary school days. The examples of how to set out work in columns of units, tens etc. are intended as a reminder for those who may have lapsed into bad habits by secondary school. Insistence on column headings is less important than checking that the numbers line up in columns, with no misalignment at the units column.

1 3969
2 321
3 96 615
4 3383
5 12 373
6 131
7 2722
8 2808
9 252
10 Seven hundred
11 Nine thousand nine hundred and eleven
12 Eighty-four
13 One thousand five hundred and fifty-seven
14 Twenty-one thousand, eight hundred and four
15 Two thousand four hundred and ninety-four
16 Eight hundred and sixty-eight thousand and nine
17 Nineteen thousand, two hundred and seventeen
18 One thousand two hundred and ninety-two

Level 4 Unit 1

19 One hundred and nine thousand, three hundred and ninety-one

20 Fifty-nine thousand, three hundred and twenty five

Exercise 1.3

The key skill in Section 1.3 is to understand the effect of multiplying or dividing by 10 or 100. The third example, 7000 × 200, sows the seed of an extension to the basic rule; this is followed up more fully in the later Level 5 work.

1	45 200	2	25 060	3	1 386 600
4	4550	5	637 000	6	2390
7	906	8	4500	9	1200

10 Nine hundred and thirty thousand

11 Sixteen thousand

12 Five thousand

13 One hundred and eighty

14 Two hundred and fifty

15 Eighty-three thousand

16 Six thousand, four hundred

17 Two hundred thousand

18 One hundred and forty

19 Four thousand, five hundred

20 Two hundred thousand

Review exercise 1

Those pupils with a talent for history might like to research a better answer to question 25*; there were periods during the Hundred Years War when hostilities ceased temporarily.
Question 30* defines a megabyte as 1000 kilobytes; in fact some computer users would define this as 1024 kilobytes instead, since this number is a power of 2.

1 a) 12 401 **b)** 65 704
  c) 63 090 **d)** 402 611
  e) 5040

2 a) Twenty-two thousand, three hundred and one
  b) Four hundred and fifty thousand, two hundred and seven
  c) Fifty thousand and fifty-six
  d) One hundred and three thousand, two hundred and forty-six
  e) Seven thousand, two hundred and nine

3 48 151   **4** 16 245
5 4472   **6** 678
7 11 001   **8** 2839
9 96 422   **10** 2159
11 45 431   **12** 600 000
13 8000   **14** 500 000
15 40   **16** 600
17 22 600 000   **18** 2260
19 700 000   **20*** 80
21* 104 496   **22*** 3777
23* a) 2100 **b)** 700
24* 230   **25*** 116 years
26* 4860   **27*** ####2#00
28* 160 000
29* 4356 francs, about £436
30* 1525 kB, which is less than 2000 kB so the files will fit.

Unit 2
Numbers and number patterns

- *This Unit could be introduced by discussing the common tests for divisibility, including:*
  divisibility by 2 – *the units digit is 0, 2, 4, 6 or 8*
  divisibility by 3 – *the sum of the digits is divisible by 3*
  divisibility by 4 – *the last two digits give a number divisible by 4*
  divisibility by 5 – *the units digit is 0 or 5*
  divisibility by 6 – *the number passes the '2' and '3' tests*
  divisibility by 8 – *the last three digits give a number divisible by 8*
  divisibility by 9 – *the sum of the digits is divisible by 9*
- *Talented pupils might be challenged to devise a test for divisibility by 7.*

Exercise 2.1

In Unit 2.1 the emphasis is on confirming knowledge of times tables up to 10 by 10. Posters can be helpful here, perhaps made by the pupils themselves.

1	32	2	30	3	9	4	14
5	25	6	12	7	30	8	24
9	49	10	36	11	18	12	63

Exercise 2.2

This section emphasises the link between factors and the times tables; frequent reference to the grid on page 8 may be helpful. Some of the questions deliberately require continuing the pattern in one of the rows, as illustrated in the second example on page 9.

1 5, 10, 15
2 3, 6, 9, 12, 15
3 9, 18, 27, 36
4 8, 16, 24
5 7, 14, 21, 28, 35, 42
6 Yes   7 No   8 Yes   9 No
10 Yes 11 Yes 12 No   13 No
14 Yes 15 No
16 1, 2, 3, 4, 6, 12   17 1, 3, 5, 15
18 1, 2, 4, 8, 16   19 1, 2, 3, 6, 9, 18
20 1, 2, 3, 5, 6, 10, 15, 30

Exercise 2.3

Once again the grid on page 8 should be used. Numbers appearing within it are composite, while the gaps indicate primes. Emphasise that the number 1 is a special case; although it is not composite it is not considered to be prime either.

1 19   2 23, 29
3 composite   4 prime
5 prime   6 59
7 41, 43, 47   8 composite
9 prime   10 composite

Level 4 Unit 2

Exercise 2.4

This section could be introduced by means of a 'spot the number' game on the board e.g. 'What comes next in the pattern 5, 7, 9, 11, …?' Emphasise that the correct answer not only supplies the missing number(s) but also contains an explanation of the rule that is being used.

1. Start at 4, go up 4 at a time.   20, 24
2. Start at 10, go up 2 at a time.   20, 22
3. Start at 6, go up 5 at a time.   26, 31
4. Start at 60, go down 5 at a time. 35, 30
5. Start at 100, go down 3 at a time. 85, 82
6. Start at 1, go up 3, then 5, then 7 etc. 36, 49 (or square numbers)
7. Start at 1, go up 9 then 1, etc.   30, 31
8. Start at 1, go up 1, then 2, then 4 etc. 32, 64 (or double each time)
9. Start at 1, go up 1, then 2, then 3 etc. 16, 22
10. 10, 15, 21, 28

Review Exercise 2

The Sieve of Eratosthenes, question 28*, is recommended as an excellent way of finishing an initial look at prime numbers and factors.

1. 18
2. 54
3. 64
4. 21
5. 32
6. 35
7. 16
8. 35
9. 48
10. 40
11. 28
12. 81
13. No
14. No
15. No
16. 1, 2, 7, 14
17. Yes
18. No
19. No
20. 1, 2, 4, 8, 16, 32
21. Start at 10, go up 3 at a time, 25
22. Start at 10, go up 3, then 4, then 5 etc., 35
23. Start at 90, go down 9 at a time, 45
24. Start at 1, go up 8, down 1 etc., 23
25. Start at 1, multiply by 3 each time, 243
26.* 43
27.* 67

Unit 3
Fractions and percentages

Exercise 3.1

*Section 3.1 introduces the terms **numerator** and **denominator**. The key point is to establish the denominator (bottom) first, by counting the number of parts in the diagram, then find the numerator (top) afterwards, by counting. Some examples on the board or OHP are a helpful introduction.*

It should be mentioned in passing that these diagrams always lead to fractions smaller than 1; in later work on fractions this need not always be so.

1 $\frac{1}{4}$ 2 $\frac{5}{8}$ 3 $\frac{5}{9}$ 4 $\frac{1}{4}$
5 $\frac{5}{8}$ 6 $\frac{7}{12}$ 7 $\frac{3}{5}$ 8 $\frac{7}{10}$
9 $\frac{1}{6}$ 10 $\frac{5}{16}$

Exercise 3.2

Section 3.2 shows how a diagram may be used to justify the equivalence of $\frac{3}{4}$ and $\frac{6}{8}$; it may be helpful to show the class how this can also be done by multiplying both 3 and 4 by the same number, in this case 2, before progressing to the second example. While the diagram is a helpful aid to understanding it is intended that Exercise 3.2 should be done by using multiplication.

1 $\frac{2}{6}$ and $\frac{3}{9}$ (there are others also)
2 $\frac{6}{14}$ and $\frac{9}{21}$ (there are others also)
3 $\frac{8}{18}$ and $\frac{12}{27}$ and $\frac{16}{36}$ (there are others also)

4 40   5 21   6 44   7 $\frac{1}{4}$
8 $\frac{2}{3}$ 9 $\frac{3}{4}$ 10 $\frac{6}{7}$

Exercise 3.3

The examples show how to build the answer up by assigning a percentage to each region in the diagram. An alternative approach would be to obtain a fraction first, e.g. $\frac{1}{4}$, then write this as the equivalent fraction $\frac{25}{100}$, hence 25%. As with Exercise 3.1, these diagrams can only lead to answers of less than 100%.

1 75%   2 60%   3 50%   4 10%
5 40%   6 60%

Review Exercise 3

1 $\frac{2}{3}$ 2 $\frac{7}{10}$ 3 $\frac{5}{6}$ 4 $\frac{1}{6}$
5 $\frac{4}{9}$ 6 $\frac{5}{12}$

7 (Any five squares should be shaded.)
8 (Any seven squares should be shaded.)
9 (Any three triangles should be shaded.)
10 (Any one sector should be shaded.)
11 $\frac{3}{5}$ 12 $\frac{3}{5}$ 13 $\frac{7}{8}$ 14 $\frac{7}{9}$
15 $\frac{3}{5}$ 16 $\frac{3}{7}$ 17 32   18 10
19 $\frac{5}{16}$ 20 $\frac{2}{3}$ 21 60%   22 90%
23 5%   24 35%   25* $\frac{4}{5}$ 26* 85%
27* Yes, 20% is the same as $\frac{1}{5}$.
28* No, 40% is the same as $\frac{4}{10}$, not $\frac{4}{9}$.
29* $\frac{2}{3}$ 30* 30%

Unit 4
Working with decimals

Exercise 4.1

This section gives a simple introduction to the relationship between simple fractions and decimals. In particular, fractions with a denominator of 10 or 100 are considered; those with less convenient denominators are deferred until later.

1 0.7 **2** 6.1 **3** 1.9 **4** 4.7
5 2.3 **6** 10.7 **7** 2.9 **8** 1.1
9 6.7 **10** 4.3 **11** 5.7 **12** 12.9
13 0.11 **14** 1.07 **15** 6.39 **16** 20.49
17 5.67 **18** 8.91 **19** 3.19 **20** 5.07

Exercise 4.2

Exercise 4.2 could be supplemented with, or indeed preceded by, a practical activity such as measuring the lengths of objects in the classroom in centimetres or millimetres, then converting the final answer to metres (so that a decimal point has to be inserted).

1 32.5 cm **2** 20.8 cm **3** 14.4 cm
4 9.1 cm **5** 2.56 m **6** 1.55 m
7 3.10 m **8** 0.13 m **9** 1.33 m
10 4.5 cm and 2.7 cm

Exercise 4.3

It may be worth demonstrating the second example on the OHP or board. Problems of alignment are easily remedied by the judicious use of extra zeroes.

1 17.9 **2** 45.3 **3** 2.1 **4** 62.8
5 3.5 **6** 27.9 **7** 6.9 **8** 113.7
9 22.11 **10** 81.09 **11** 13.32
12 51.29 **13** 54.19 **14** 33.24
15 9.46 **16** £24.98 **17** £18.01
18 £2.84 **19** £32.49 **20** £16.99

Review Exercise 4

Pupils may be unfamiliar with the notation used in question 11*, despite the example given.
Discussion: 'Can you think of other examples where decimal notation is used in everyday life?'

1 a) 3.1 **b)** 4.61 **c)** 5.04
2 a) 1.1 **b)** 1.01 **c)** 1.11
   d) 4.17 **e)** 2.71
3 a) 16.4 cm **b)** 9.1 cm **c)** 121 cm
   d) 77 cm **e)** 2 cm
4 25.2 **5** 19.2 **6** 19.63
7 48.28 **8** 3.01 **9** 25.2
10 13.99 **11*** 35.2 km
12* a) £42.56 **b)** £7.44
13* a) £15.80 **b)** £5.26 or £5.27
14* a) 1.7 m **b)** 70 cm
15* a) 56.8 km **b)** 14.2 km

Unit 5
Coordinates

Exercise 5.1

The key point is that a pair of numbers may be used to specify the position of a point on plane. In introducing this topic, check that the pupils understand what is actually meant by 'a plane'.

A common error is to use (20, 50) when they mean (50, 20); stories such as 'you go along the street first before you up to the tenth floor of an office block' can prove helpful.

The activity (question 4) can illustrate how an elegant mathematical concept does not always work quite so well in practice, e.g. in an oddly-shaped classroom.

1 **a)** (4, 3)   **b)** (3, 2)   **c)** (2, 4)
2 **a)** Cave   **b)** (10, 40)   **c)** (30, 50)
   d) (30, 20) or (50, 40)
3 **a)** Renault   **b)** BMW
   c) (1, 1), (1, 4), (1, 6), (2, 2), (2, 6), (3, 2), (3, 5), (4, 2), (4, 4), (4, 6)

Exercise 5.2

When plotting axes and points, watch for the 'battleships' players who like to label the middle of the squares with 1, 2, 3, etc. rather than the grid lines. Be careful about drawing too many analogies with maps: at the end of the day a set of coordinates describes a mathematical point, whereas a six-figure OS grid reference describes an area of 10 000 square metres of land!

1 It is a square.
2 It is a rectangle. M is at (4, 2).
3 X is at (3, 1).
4 C could be at (4, 5).
5 It is a sailing boat.

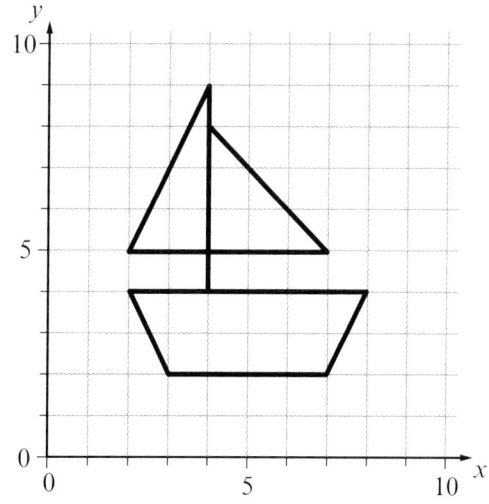

7

Level 4 Unit 5

Review Exercise 5

Most of these are straightforward questions giving further practice on coordinates. Question 5* could be developed into a class competition, with a prize for the best entry.

1. **a)** C (1, 4), D (4, 5), E (5, 2)
   b) G
2. The name TIM should be spelt out.
3. The name VAL is spelt out.
4. The name ALEX is spelt out.
5.

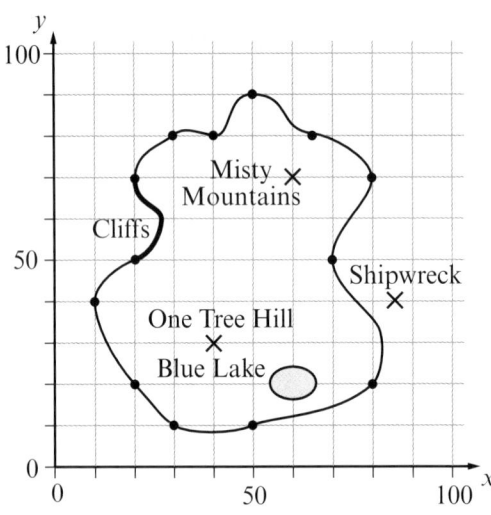

Unit 6
2-D shapes and 3-D models

Exercise **6.1**

Many pupils find it helpful to have a small mirror, perhaps made out of mirror card, available for this topic. Those who have difficulty in copying diagrams accurately onto squared paper might need to work from prepared photocopy diagrams, at least to begin with.

1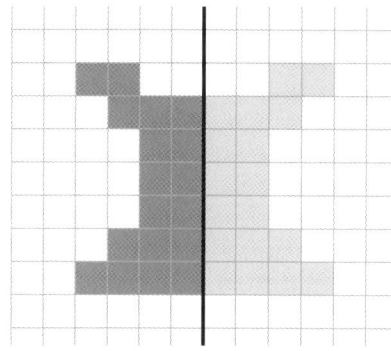

2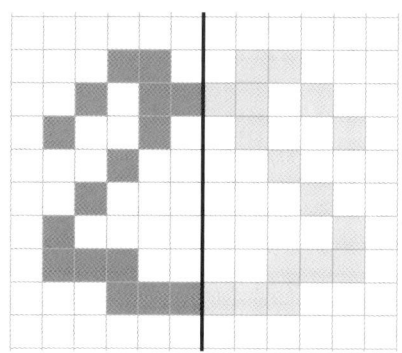

3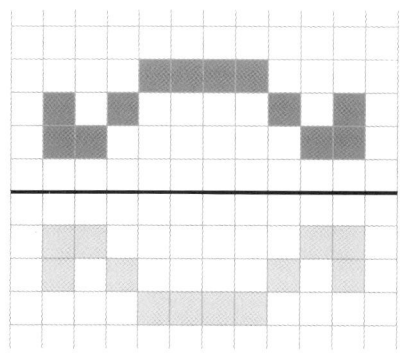

4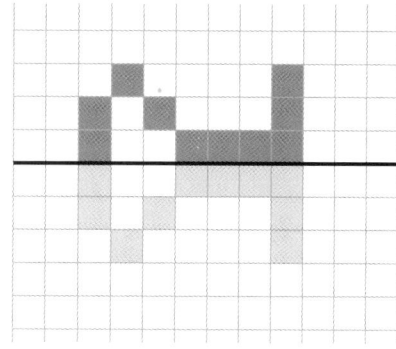

5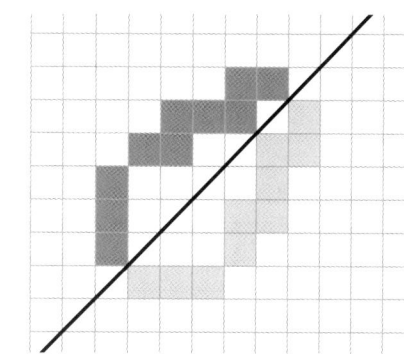

6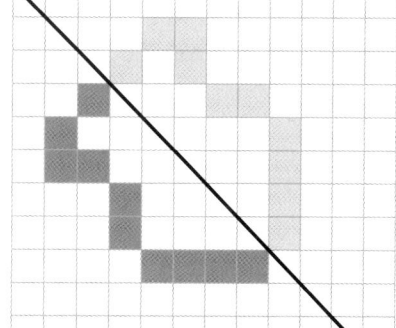

Exercise **6.2**

Some pupils find order of rotational symmetry extremely difficult to visualise, others find it trivial. Tracing paper might be helpful in this section, though it is often easier to rotate the book instead!

1 Order 4 **2** Order 2 **3** Order 4
4 Order 2 **5** Order 3 **6** Order 5

9

Level 4 Unit 6

Exercise 6.3

Tracing paper might be helpful in this section, or 'Digifix' cubes could be used to make models of the shapes in question 3.

1 A and D   **2** B and E
3 a) J **b)** G **c)** H **d)** B

Exercise 6.4

This section could be extended to include more model-making activities, using cardboard nets. Alternatively a kit of plastic shape such as 'Polydron' can be used to good effect; this has the added advantage that pupils with weak craft skills are still able to make good mathematical models.

1 Four (equilateral) triangles
2 Six squares
3 Twelve pentagons

Review Exercise 6

The pop-up dodecahedron activity (question 6*) is recommended as a fun way of concluding this topic. Careful experimentation with the rubber band is needed in order to find one that is just the right length; if in doubt, use bands that are too long so they can be broken and knotted.

1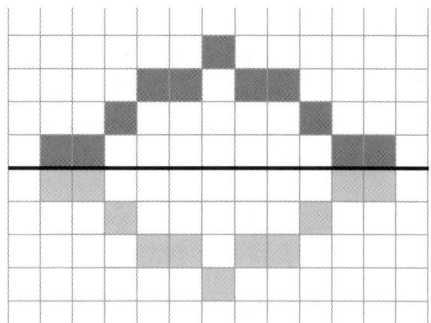

2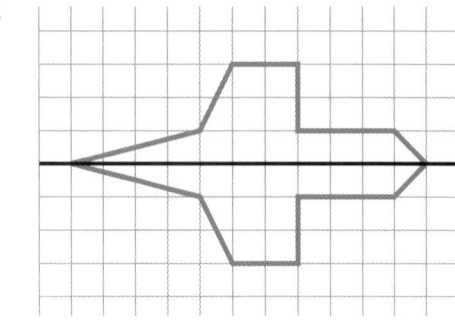

3 a) I, O, H, S
   b) I, O, V, E, M, A, T, H
   c) L
4 Henry is not right. For example, his sides could be 5, 5, 1 and Madge's could be 5, 5, 2.
5* A, B and H all make cubes.

Unit 7
Units and scales

Exercise 7.1

Some introductory work on the prefixes centi-, milli- and kilo- is useful; those with appetites for large numbers might go on to mega-, giga- etc., though opportunities for practice with everyday metric units are then a little restricted. Although time units do not go up in powers of ten they are included in this Unit, since the second is the standard metric unit of time. Time is, interestingly, a rare example of a case in which metric and imperial units are identical.

Watch for pupils brought up on a diet of centimetres and metres – they make the common slip of regarding a kilogram as 100 grams, or a litre as 100 millilitres.

1 15 cm 5 mm **2** 1 day 7 hours
3 1 kg 350 g **4** 2 m 88 cm
5 5 min 20 s

Exercise 7.2

There are no 'right answers' to this exercise, although the units given for question 1 seem to be the most sensible. The suggested answers for question 2 are precisely that – suggestions – and it is likely that pupil answers will vary significantly from these.

1 a) metres
   b) grams
   c) centimetres (or millimetres)
   d) litres
   e) minutes
   f) tonnes
   g) millilitres (or centilitres)
   h) millimetres
   i) kilograms
   j) kilometres

(These are only suggestions.)

2 a) 1 metre
   b) 100 tonnes
   c) 4 kilograms
   d) 8 millimetres
   e) 350 millilitres
   f) 50 grams
   g) 10 centimetres
   h) 60 litres
   i) 20 centimetres
   j) 1 litre

Exercise 7.3

This exercise should be supported by practical classroom activities on weighing and measuring. It is this author's belief that problems involving units of length are usually solved more accurately than those involving weight, while capacity is done worst of all, probably because a litre is harder to visualise than a metre. Opportunities to weigh objects, and measure the capacity of a container (using measuring cylinders etc.) should be provided whenever appropriate.

1 6.65   **2** 5.8   **3** 10.4
4 5.75   **5** 12.8 **6** 5
7 38.5   **8** $12\frac{7}{8}$ **9** 58 mph
10 8500

11

Level 4 Unit 7

Review Exercise 7

1. 2 cm 5 mm
2. 1 kg 200 g
3. 2 h 50 min
4. 4 m 80 cm
5. 150 min
6. 330 s
7. 6300 g
8. 1004 cm
9. 126 h
10. 11050 ml
11. metres
12. millimetres
13. grams
14. litres
15. minutes

(The answers to 16 to 20 are only suggestions.)

16. 25 m
17. 10 litres
18. 3 kg
19. 1 h
20. 4 mm
21. 188 cm (or 187, or 187.5)
22. 46.6°
23. 36.25
24. 40.65
25. 1500

Unit 8
Perimeter, area and volume

In this Unit some answers will be exact (since they are found by counting grid squares) while others are approximate (the result of measuring). Approximate answers need to be rounded to a sensible degree of accuracy.

Exercise 8.1

1 14 cm   2 20 cm   3 26 cm
4 22 cm   5 20 cm   6 18 cm

(The answers to 7 to 10 are only approximate, as they involve measurement.)

7 10.6 cm   8 10.0 cm   9 12.5 cm
10 15.2 cm

Exercise 8.2

Check that pupils recognise the equivalent notations for area: square centimetres, sq cm and cm^2 may all be encountered.

1 6 cm^2 2 9 cm^2 3 12 cm^2
4 10 cm^2 5 9 cm^2 6 8 cm^2

Exercise 8.3

Watch for pupils who overestimate areas by counting small part-squares as full. The concept of 'at least half full' is actually surprisingly hard to use in practice.

(The answers to 1 to 4 are only approximate, as they involve estimation.)

1 45 cm^2 2 36 cm^2 3 27 cm^2
4 36 cm^2

Exercise 8.4

Check that pupils recognise the equivalent notations for volume: cubic centimetres and cm^3 may both be encountered, but the old-fashioned 'cc' (as in a 250cc motorbike) ought now to be discouraged. Volumes may also be expressed in litres, but should be discouraged here as the emphasis of this entire Unit is on the progression from linear to square to cubic units.

1 18 cm^3 2 9 cm^3 3 18 cm^3
4 14 cm^3 5 10 cm^3 6 17 cm^3

Review Exercise 8

1 24 cm, 31 cm^2 2 20 cm, 15 cm^2
3 26 cm, 24 cm^2 4 32 cm, 22 cm^2
5 34 cm, 28 cm^2 6 20 cm, 9 cm^2
7 4.5 + 4.5 + 2.3 = 11.3 cm
8 3.3 + 2.4 + 3.3 + 2.4 = 11.4 cm
9 9.6 cm   10 15.8 cm   11 52 cm^2
12 32 cm^2 13 50 cm^2 14 30 cm^2
15 24 cm^3 16 15 cm^3 17 16 cm^3
18 20 cm^3 19* 10 m^3, 34 m^2
20* a)   b) 8 cm^3
         c) 4 cm^2

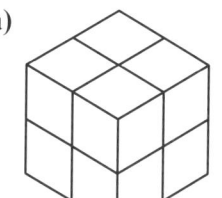

Level 4 Unit 8

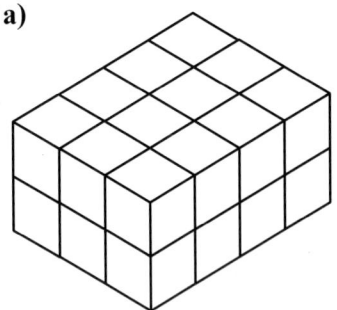

21* a)

    b) 24 cm^3
    c) 6 cm^2, 8 cm^2 and 12 cm^2

22* a) $3 \times 3 \times 3 = 27$ and $4 \times 4 \times 4 = 64$.
    30 is not a perfect cube.
    b) 2 cm by 3 cm by 5 cm
    c) 30 cm^3
    d) 62 cm^2

Unit 9
Looking at data

Exercise 9.1

The mode and median are two quite different concepts, but they both aim to describe the 'typical' member of a set of data. Thus they are treated together in the same section, but pupils need to be aware of the distinction between them.
*At this level all median calculations are based on an **odd** number of data points, so that the middle number may be readily identified. The procedure for an even number of points is described in Level 5 work (e.g. page 121, section 18.2).*

1. Mode 23, median 27
2. Mode 24, median 22
3. 2
4. Mode 12, median 12
5. 11

Exercise 9.2

A common mistake in drawing up tally charts is to scan for all the 6s first, then all the 7s etc: this invariably leads to numbers being left out. It is a good idea to introduce this topic by doing some examples on the OHP or board, ticking off the data points from the beginning of the list to the end. Many pupils (but not all) should be familiar with the idea of tying up bundles of 5 tallies.

1a)

Amount	0	10	20	50
Frequency	3	6	5	3

b)

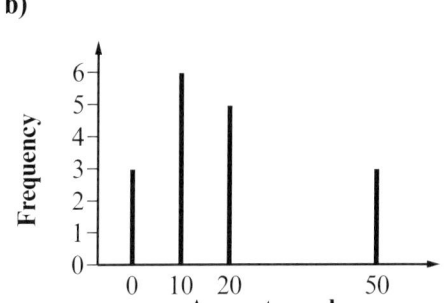

2 a)

Score	3	4	5	6	7	8	9	10
Frequency	2	1	2	3	5	6	9	2

b) The mode is 9.

c)

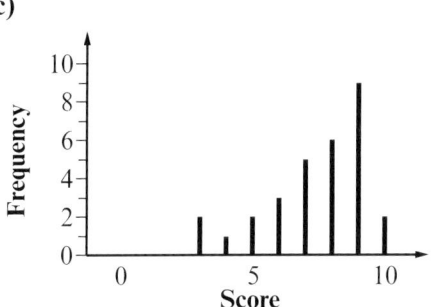

3 a)

Score	1	2	3	4	5	6
Frequency	4	3	6	3	4	4

b)

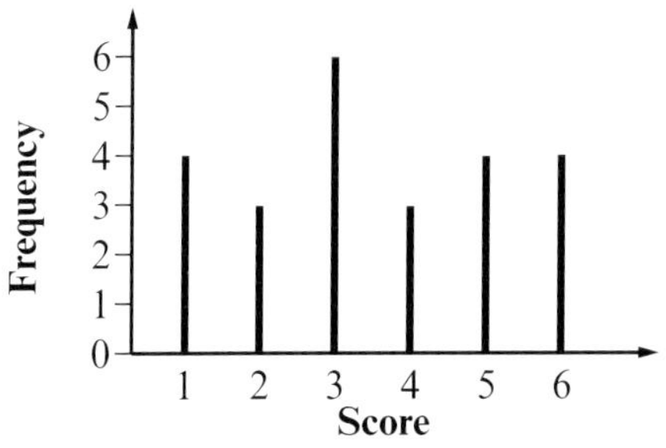

c) The mode is 3.

Level 4 Unit 9

4 a) The mode is 51 matches.
 b)

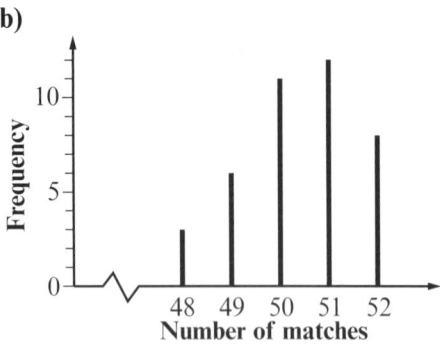

 c) The claim does seem reasonable, as most of the boxes contain 50 matches or more.

5 a)

Number of times	0	1	2	3	4	5
Frequency	10	16	15	4	5	0

 b) The mode is 1.
 c)

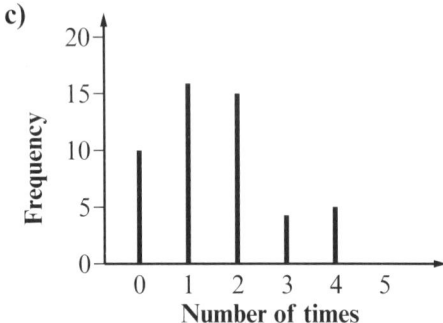

Exercise 9.3

This topic is a potential minefield of misunderstanding! At this level the data sets are discrete, but take too many different values for simple tallying to be effective; they are thus grouped into (discrete) intervals, where the top end of one interval differs by 1 from the bottom end of the next interval.

*The diagram shown in the example on page 62 has been labelled with **categories** along the x-axis, rather than numbers, to avoid problems with half-units and gaps. The diagram is, in effect, a halfway house between the simple vertical line graph (Section 9.2) and the more sophisticated treatment of continuous data which lies ahead (Unit 31, e.g. page 236).*

1 a)

Mark	Frequency
0–4	6
5–9	7
10–14	4
15–19	3
20–24	4
25–29	1

 b)

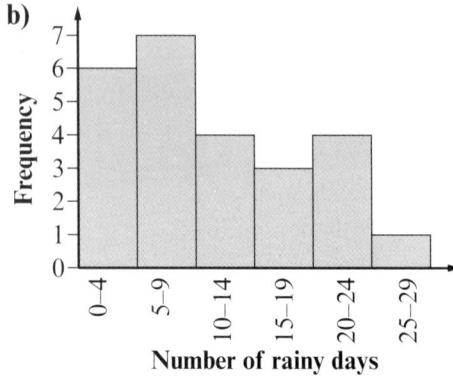

 c) The modal group is 5–9 days

2 a)

Mark	Frequency
00–09	0
10–19	2
20–29	0
30–39	6
40–49	10
50–59	16
60–69	5
70–79	8
80–89	2
90–99	1

Level 4 Unit 9

b)

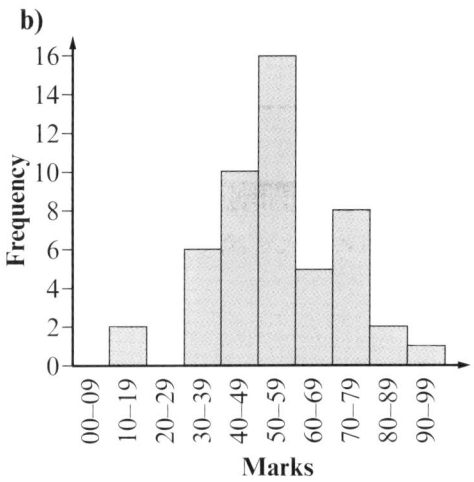

c) The modal group is 50–59 marks.
d) 23 candidates passed.

3 a)

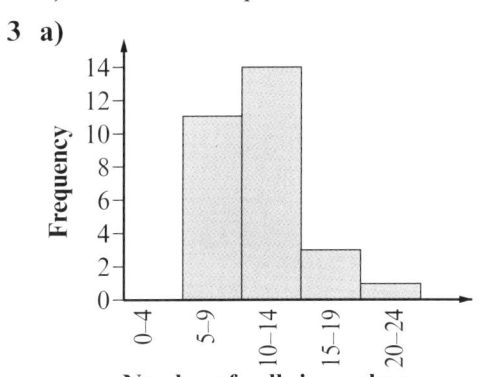

b) The modal class is 10–14 hours.
c) The data represents 29 hours altogether.
d) 5 calls

Review Exercise 9

1 a) 7   b) 6   c) 2
2 a) No mode   b) 7   c) 2
3 a) 2   b) 1
4 a) 4   b) 4
5 a) 1   b) 0
6 a)

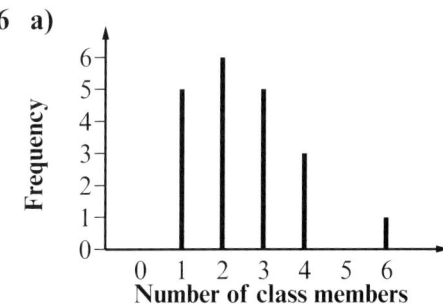

b) The mode is 2.
c) 5 occasions

7 a)

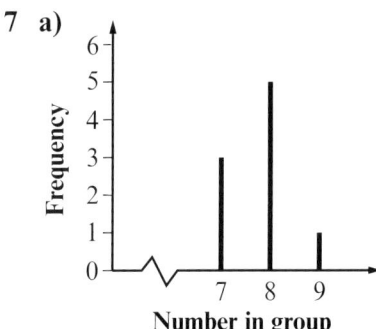

b) 8   c) 8   d) 70 people

8* There are infinitely many alternative answers. Here is one possible set:
a) 2 3 4 7 7
b) 2 2 8 9 10
c) 1 2 3 4 4
d) 1 2 2 2 3

9* 2 2 5 8 9 9 9

10* a) 1 pet   b) 0 pets
c) The median is better, as it is not 0.

17

Unit 10
Introducing probability

Exercise 10.1

The purpose of this introductory section is simply to identify situations where probability applies, i.e. to distinguish between situations with only one possible outcome and those where more than one outcome is possible.

1. Certain
2. Uncertain
3. Uncertain
4. Certain
5. Uncertain
6. Certain
7. Uncertain
8. Uncertain
9. Certain
10. Certain

Exercise 10.2

This section builds on the previous one by beginning to assign measures of likelihood to the outcome of a probability experiment.

1. a) Unlikely
   b) Even chance
   c) Likely
2. a) Likely
   b) Impossible
   c) Unlikely
   d) Even chance
3. a) Yes
   b) No

Review Exercise 10

1. a) Likely
   b) Even chance
   c) Unlikely
   d) Unlikely
2. a) Even chance
   b) Impossible
   c) Unlikely
3* Four purple faces, one yellow, one green
4* a) 4
   b) Yes: they must not be red!
5* a) 8
   b) 5

Level 4
Review

Exercise 1
1. 6705
2. 70 241
3. Two thousand, one hundred and seven
4. Thirty-four thousand and sixty
5. 3520
6. 560 000
7. 4300
8. 1080
9. 9, 18, 27, 36, 45
10. No
11. 1, 2, 4, 5, 10, 20
12. No
13. 23 (or 29)
14. Yes
15. 2.9
16. 6.49
17. $2\frac{7}{10}$
18. $\frac{3}{5}$
19. 5
20. $\frac{5}{12}$

Exercise 2
1. 54
2. 3
3. 4 cm 5 mm
4. 6045 g
5. grams
6. metres
7. a) 6.6 km   b) Petra is right.
8. 21
9. False
10. 10.3

Exercise 3
1. 903
2. 32 488
3. 362
4. 92
5. £18.15
6. £3.80
7. a) 31, 34
   b) 29, 23
   c) 160, 320
8. a) 34.5 cm
   b) 345 mm
9. a) 3 h 15 min
   b) 195 min
10. a) (2, 5)
    b) (1, 2)
11. 4
12. Penny is right.
13. 11
14. a) 20 pages
    b) The mode is 3 mistakes.
15. Regular hexagon
16. Rhombus
17. Cube
18. Square-based pyramid
19. a) 32 m
    b) 28 m^2
    c) 61 m^2

Level 5 Unit 11
Decimals and negative numbers

Exercise 11.1

The key point in this section is that numbers must align at the decimal point, and therefore not necessarily at the right hand end. To avoid untidy ends it is often useful to insert an extra zero, as shown in the second example on page 74. Pupils who find this whole topic difficult might require further practice just on addition before progressing to questions involving subtraction, although the underlying concept of place value is identical in both cases.

1. a) 16.742   b) 105.2   c) 10.006
2. a) Sixty-nine point two five
   b) One hundred and eighty-four point nought six
   c) Twenty-one point nought six nought
3. 41.24   4. 396.23   5. 437.26
6. 383.692   7. 63.63   8. 81.77
9. 183.03   10. 66.52   11. 112.695
12. 581.93   13. 9.84   14. 424.19
15. 23.577   16. 0.28

Exercise 11.2

Pupils need to distinguish between problems which do not need a calculator (× 200, ÷ 50 etc.) and those which do (÷ 135.6). The projected development of calculator-free papers as part of both GCSE and A-level emphasise the importance of practising calculator-free skills during Key Stage 3.

1. 150.68   2. 693.06   3. 72.34
4. 318.128   5. 484.5   6. 3510
7. 9.007   8. 12 644.8   9. 9.814
10. 783.75   11. 22.27   12. 2.56
13. 9.85   14. 59.908   15. 2.8
16. 2.68   17. 1719.63   18. 1.565 12

Exercise 11.3

Beware of simple rules such as 'two minuses make a plus' – while it is true that $(-2) \times (-3) = +6$ there is scope for confusion with $(-2) + (-3) = -5$, in which 'two minuses make an even bigger minus.' The concept recommended in this section is that the basic process of adding a positive number moves you to the right; the full set of rules for negative numbers are set out in the notes on pages 76 and 77.

1. −4, −3, 6
2. −7, −3, 10
3. −3.5, 1.4, 3.5
4. −7.5, −7.33, 14.05, 14.66
5. −0.32, −0.310, 0.05, 0.6
6. −4   7. −11   8. 3   9. −7
10. −2   11. 11   12. 1   13. −1.2
14. 2   15. 16   16. −2.9   17. −5.6
18. 5.37   19. 260°C
20. a) Monday
    b) Tuesday
    c) Wednesday, by 2°C

Level 5 Unit 11

Exercise 11.4

Despite the pupils' everyday familiarity with problems involving money, failure to quote to two decimal places is often seen, e.g. £3.5 instead of £3.50. Watch also for answers such as £3.26p which tend to be heavily penalised by examiners; correct notation is £3.26 or 326p.

1 £7.76	2 £7.92	3 £6.70
4 £9.25	5 £35.05	6 £267.84
7 £5.84	8 £6.36	9 £1.68
10 £8.53		

Review Exercise 11

Problems in context often refer to 'overdraft' or 'overdrawn'; while most teachers are familiar with these terms we should not assume that all pupils understand them. Check that those who wish to try question 36* understand the vocabulary.

1 72.91	2 168.01	3 39.24
4 141.05	5 21.47	6 25.63
7 172.7	8 641.12	9 78.39
10 1774.386	11 0.9256	12 1.74
13 7.52	14 86.78	15 0.09
16 42.5	17 1.2	18 2.9445
19 7	20 −7	21 20
22 −11	23 16	24 0
25 4	26 11	27 −15

28* £11.37   29* 12 weeks
30* 7.26 m   31* Les Arcs
32* 17°C
33* a) 15°C   b) −9°C   c) 24°C
34* Highest: Val Thorens. Southernmost: Pra Loup
35* 5 hours
36* £37.46
37* $17.55

Unit 12
Multiplication and division without a calculator

■ *The success of this entire Unit depends on total familiarity with the times tables, up to 10 × 10. Some revision of work from Unit 2 could provide a useful introduction, and pupils might like to construct a number grid like that on page 8.*

Exercise 12.1

1 3325   2 15 228   3 10 686
4 14 949   5 20 150   6 3478
7 7107   8 31 744   9 73 944
10 24 948   11 39 567   12 38 415
13 60 600   14 37 179   15 36 450
16 81 006   17 243 873   18 329 308
19 50 625   20 52 668

Exercise 12.2

Long division can be a source of anxiety, but the preparation of a list of multiples, as in the example on page 82, removes many potential difficulties and is time well spent.
While calculators normally express the remainder as a decimal the remainders in this section are left either as whole numbers or expressed as fractions of the original divisor. Watch for opportunities to cancel here.

1 2377   2 5284
3 259 r 10   4 3266 r 3
5 3177   6 4283 r 16
7 788 r 7   8 24 655 r 27
9 275   10 226
11 $381\frac{13}{29}$ 12 $148\frac{17}{53}$
13 $244\frac{6}{41}$ 14 $385\frac{58}{77}$
15 $1725\frac{12}{31}$ 16 $958\frac{7}{24}$
17 $377\frac{11}{31}$ 18 999

Review Exercise 12

1 35   2 40   3 18
4 72   5 32   6 12
7 6   8 11   9 8
10 7   11 44   12 49
13 7   14 12   15 36
16 11   17 144   18 8
19 8   20 132   21 1905
22 5440   23 10 032   24 16 854
25 52 542   26 521 203   27 45
28 421   29 771   30 617
31 322 r 7   32 4427 r 8
33 384 players   34 643 passengers
35* a) £27.36 b) £59.52   c) £86.88
36* a) £7.11   b) £2.89
37* 479 001 600
38* 19 or 20 pupils
39* 24
40* a) 17, 34, 51, . . . ,289, 306, 323, 340
    b) 19, 38, 57, . . . ,323, 342, 361, 380
    c) 323

Unit 13
Fractions and percentages

- The initial section gives practice at finding a simple fraction of a given amount. At this stage the use of a calculator could be allowed for those who lack confidence with basic multiplication and division, but pupils using a calculator should be encouraged to do the division first. Although the order does not affect the final answer, the intermediate numbers are kept more manageable in this way.
- Use of a calculator key $a\frac{b}{c}$ is not to be encouraged at this stage, as this does conceal the underlying principles of the arithmetic.

Exercise 13.1

1	15	2	132	3	38	4	80
5	3894	6	70	7	2492	8	8
9	93	10	1068	11	352	12	305
13	875	14	724	15	110	16	48
17	46	18	145	19	259	20	192

Exercise 13.2

The examples show how to use 1% as a halfway house, and how to recognise standard simple fractions. An alternative strategy based on equivalent fractions might work well here also.

1	630	2	18	3	180
4	17.6	5	30	6	48
7	$420	8	£27	9	£1250
10	2700 people			11	324
12	$678	13	600	14	108
15	£2880	16	£50	17	725
18	108	19	9.6	20	9.6

Exercise 13.3

Easy examples like $\frac{11}{50}$ lend themselves nicely to an alternative approach based on equivalent fractions, but this works less effectively with awkward amounts like $\frac{9}{11}$, where a calculator method is perhaps best.

1	37.5%	2	66.7%	3	90%
4	15%	5	70%	6	62.5%
7	7.5%	8	36.4%	9	5%
10	71.4%	11	81.8%	12	77.8%
13	28%	14	41.7%	15	13.3%
16	22%	17	14%	18	76%
19	96%	20	93.3%		

Exercise 13.4

Here the use of a calculator key $a\frac{b}{c}$ could be endorsed, provided enough examples are done by hand first so that the fairly straightforward arithmetic principle has been clearly understood.

| 1 | $\frac{8}{25}$ | 2 | $\frac{1}{25}$ | 3 | $\frac{11}{25}$ | 4 | $\frac{4}{25}$ |
| 5 | $\frac{7}{50}$ | 6 | $\frac{9}{50}$ | 7 | $\frac{1}{40}$ | 8 | $\frac{61}{100}$ |

Level 5 Unit 13

9 $\frac{99}{100}$ 10 $\frac{4}{5}$ 11 $\frac{1}{20}$ 12 $\frac{7}{40}$
13 $\frac{1}{2}$ 14 $\frac{3}{20}$ 15 $\frac{11}{20}$ 16 $\frac{43}{50}$
17 $\frac{13}{50}$ 18 $\frac{19}{100}$ 19 $\frac{1}{6}$ 20 $\frac{1}{8}$

Review Exercise 13

1 450   2 896
3 36 million   4 48
5 108   6 55
7 108   8 84
9 $30   10 £78.75
11 £160   12 75 people
13 4100 m   14 300 litres
15 £280   16 676 kg
17 $40.95   18 570 cm
19 5950 m   20 53 760 lire
21 a) Smallest: 20%, largest: two-fifths
   b) Smallest: 43%, largest: 50%
   c) Smallest: 65%, largest: five-sevenths
22 £275.60   23 1320 yards
24 Cheapskate: £23.33
   Bargain: £25.00
   Cost Less £22.75
   The best deal is at Cost Less.
25 5320 pounds   26 Mathematics
27 880 square yards 28 42 items
29* 387 pupils   30* 20%, $\frac{1}{5}$
31* 300 children 32* 2016 francs
33* 37.5%
34* a) 90   b) $\frac{1}{6}$
35* £333.88
36* a) 420 mm   b) 441 mm
37* a) £106   b) £112.36
    c) £119.10   d) 12 years
38* a) 256 megabytes
    b) 20.0%

24

Unit 14
Rounding and estimation

Exercise 14.1

Some classes may benefit from seeing a very large number of examples first, on the OHP or board, to ensure that the concept of significant figures is fully understood before doing the exercises. Beware of showing misleading illustrations, such as '2600 has 2 significant figures' when in fact it might have 3 or 4; a much safer approach is to start with known figures and then round them off as in the examples on page 92.

1	160	2	25 000
3	600	4	180 000
5	450	6	32 000
7	1 500 000	8	210 000
9	40 000	10	300
11	1000	12	100
13	70 000	14	70 000
15	2 000 000	16	4000

Exercise 14.2

Emphasise that 'estimate' does not mean 'guess'. A KS3 or GCSE examiner will expect to see working to justify how the estimate has been made.

1 $60 \times 20 = 1200$
2 $400 \times 30 = 12\,000$
3 $50 \times 20 = 1000$
4 $400 \times 90 = 36\,000$
5 $5000 \div 50 = 100$
6 $400 \div 20 = 20$
7 $6000 \div 30 = 200$
8 $800 \times 800 = 640\,000$
9 $2000 \div 40 = 50$
10 $70\,g \times 20 = 1400\,g$
11 £3000 × 20 = £60 000
12 $400 \div 10 = 40$
13 $80 \div 4 = 20$
14 $200 \times 30 = 6000$
15 £600 000 ÷ 30 = £20 000
16 £5 × 10 = £50
17 $500 \div 20 = 25$
18 $40\,000 \div 200 = 200$
19 $20 \times 30 = 600$

Exercise 14.3

Small slips in pressing the keys while using a calculator often result in enormous errors! If an answer is clearly absurd this can be detected by doing a rough estimate first, so that the reasonableness of the calculator answer can be checked.

1	Correct	2	Should be 363
3	Should be 11 232	4	Correct
5	Correct	6	Correct
7	Should be 755	8	Should be 59
9	Correct	10	Should be 441

Review Exercise 14

1	54 000	2	2000
3	210	4	2 500 000
5	7000	6	4500
7	560	8	7800
9	3300	10	10 000
11	64 300	12	400

Level 5 Unit 14

13 60 000   14 3000
15 106 000   16 5000
17 11 450   18 190 000
19 10 million 20 12 000; 11 592
21 30; 24   22 60; 66
23 20 000; 35 136   24 1200; 1205.4
25 1200; 1194.25   26 1; 1.3
27 75; 76.2   28 1000; 1140.91

29* Not really: 12 + 14 + 25 is less than 61.

30* 60 + 60 + 20 + 50 = 190 which is much less than 260.

31* 20 + 60 + 10 + 20 + 50 = 160 fish

32* 200 + 40 + 80 + 100 + 20 + 30 = 470 so the box file is large enough.

33* 4000 g, or 4 kg

34* 320 000 people, which is less than a million.

35* 40 bags

36* $2000 million (i.e. $2 billion)

37* 60 × 4 = 240 and 30 × 2 = 60, so about 300 legs in total.

38* a) 365 days, 24 hours in a day, 60 minutes in an hour, 60 seconds in a minute
    b) 28 800 000 seconds
    c) 31 536 000 seconds

Level 5 Unit 18

b)

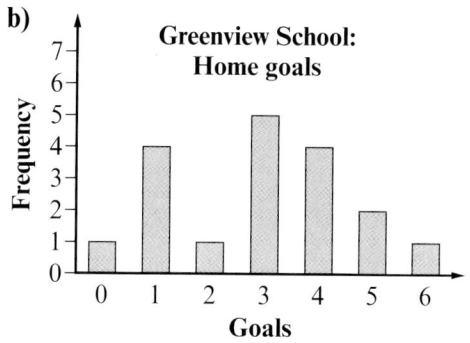

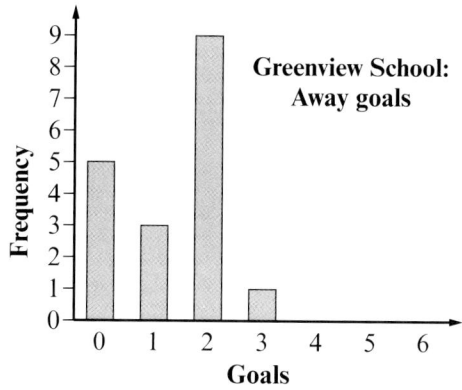

c) The average number of goals scored at home is higher than away, and the range at home is also greater.

Review Exercise 18

1. a) 5.8, 8   b) 112.2, 20
   c) 6.8875, 2.2   d) 8.4, 9
   e) 5.22, 5.8   f) 3, 5
   g) 0.5, 10   h) 90, 12

2. a) Median 3, mode 3
   b) Median 5.5, bimodal, 4 and 5
   c) Median 2, bimodal, 1 and 3
   d) Median 43, no mode
   e) Median 6, mode 8
   f) Median 99, no mode
   g) Median 10, no mode
   h) Median 77, bimodal, 77 and 81

3.

Letter	a	b	c	d	e	f	g	h	i
Frequency	11	2	2	4	13	2	4	6	10

Letter	j	k	l	m	n	o	p	q	r
Frequency	0	1	5	3	9	7	1	0	7

Letter	s	t	u	v	w	x	y	z
Frequency	9	12	4	2	2	0	4	0

a) The modal letter is e.
b) There is no mean because the letters are categories – they do not have values.

4. a)

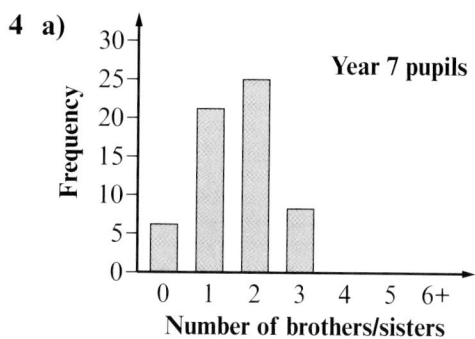

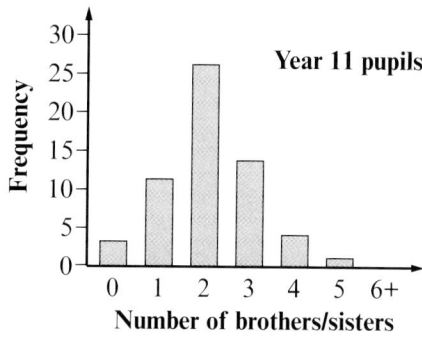

b) The Year 11 graph shows a wider range and also a greater average number of brothers and sisters.

5. a) 26 cars
   b) 3 previous owners
   c) 2.46 previous owners

Level 5 Unit 18

6 Vinay is wrong: the means are almost identical. The large value of 17 could be due to one unusually long word. Also his samples may not be representative of the two centuries.

7 a) 371 **b)** 362
  c) Galli: 90; Amerikan: 220; Capriolo: 200; Cassana: 264

8* a) Damian: 58.25; Lois: 62.25; Richard: 54.5
  b) Mathematics: 66.3; English: 41.3; French: 72.7; Science: 53
  c) 73
  d) English

9* a) 8 tracks
  b) 12.4 tracks
  c) 10.75 tracks

10* a) Volatile Chemicals (137p)
  b) Ranges are similar, but Goy-Goy has a higher mean

11* 37

12* a) John took the mean of 80 pence and £1.00. This does not work because the numbers of boys and girls are different.
  b) $(80 \times 10 + 100 \times 15) \div 25 = 92$ pence
  c) 90 pence

13* Catherine is wrong. For example, the numbers 1, 2, 4, 4, 5 have a mode of 4 but a mean of only 3.2.

14* a) The missing reading is 3 oktas.
  b) The mode is 3 oktas.

15* a) 5 and 7
  b) The median is 5 eggs.

16* a) 31 days
  b) 31 days
  c) 30.5 days
  d) The mean becomes 30.42 days.

Unit 19
Charts and line graphs

Exercise 19.1

Pupils who find difficulty in constructing accurate circles may benefit from the use of a pre-prepared grid of blank pie charts. Alternatively, trace around the outside of a protractor to obtain a convenient circle – but watch out: the classic protractor is slightly more than a semicircle.
Pie chart scales can be useful in certain special circumstances – though for the problems in this Unit it is just as easy to scale the total to 360 as it is to 100.

1 54°

2 144°

3 Angles: cola 144°, lemonade 108°, orange 78°, other drinks 30°

4 Angles: books 180°, photocopying 96°, classroom equipment 48°, staff training 15°, other 21°

5 Angles: 2p 120°, 5p 104°, 10p 84°, 1p 28°, foreign 24°

6 Angles: sleeping 120°, practising 75°, eating 60°, other 60°, teaching 45°

7 Angles: clothes 162°, toiletries 108°, savings 54°, stationery 36°

8 Angles: dogs 153°, cats 99°, hamsters 45°, lizards 36°, others 27°

9 a) 120 pupils
   b) 111°
   c) 27 pupils

10 a) Tennis looks much larger than it actually is, since it is near the front of the diagram. Similarly skiing looks smaller than it actually is, because it is towards the rear.
   b) Angles: cricket 148°, tennis 101°, netball 50°, hockey 36°, skiing 25°.

c) People who work in advertising, marketing, politics etc. who might want to make the data look more favourable than it actually is.

Exercise 19.2

Both types of graph are very easy to construct. The central point of this section is to decide which is the more suitable diagram: vertical line (discrete) or time series (continuous). If in doubt, stop and think 'Does it make sense to read off in-between values?'.

1 Line graph

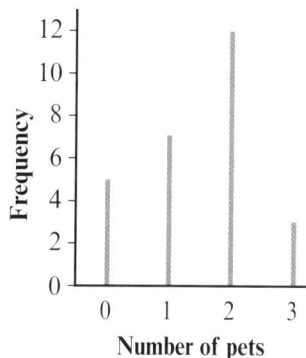

2 Time series graph

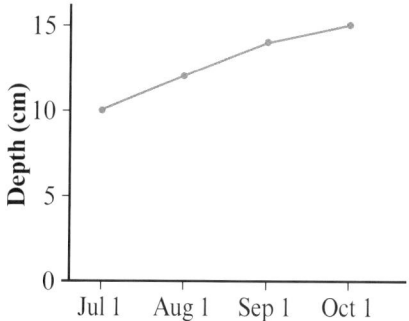

3 Line graph

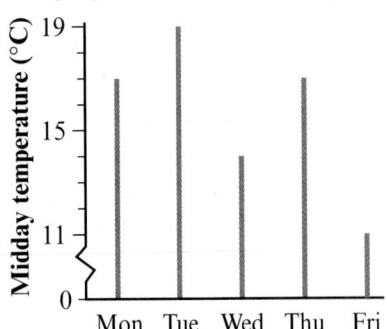

4 Time series graph

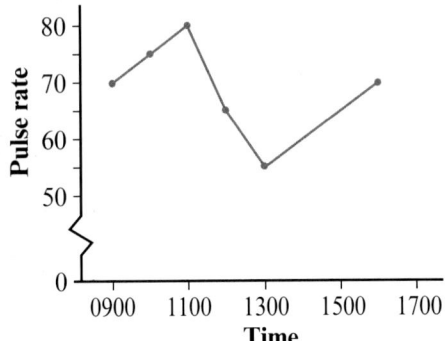

5 Line graph

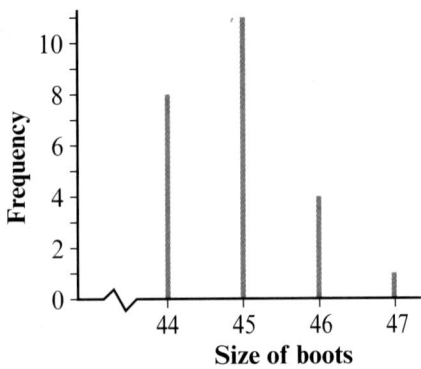

6 Line graph

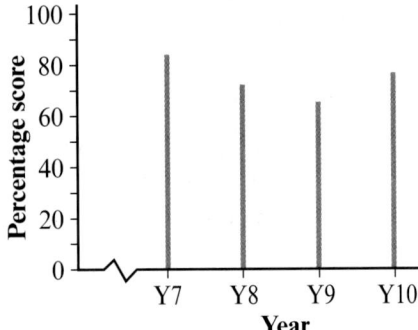

7 'Page number' cannot take values in between 0 and 1, or 1 and 2, so there should not be a continuous line running across the page. A vertical line graph is better:

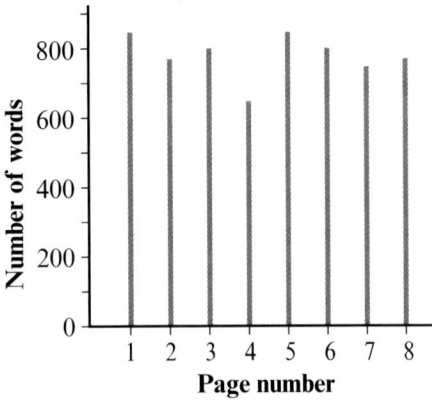

8 The 'suppression of the origin' causes the vertical scale to look exaggerated, and this gives the impression of a dramatic boom in spending. The true picture is seen when the vertical scale is allowed to run all the way down to zero:

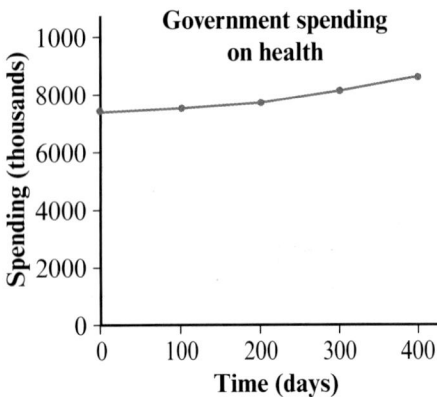

Exercise 19.3

Pictograms are easy, but watch for the pupil who draws 24 symbols to represent 24 monkeys!

A good way of making stacked bar charts is to use a computer package such as Excel.

1

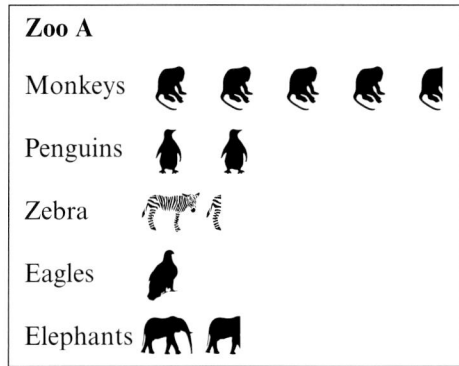

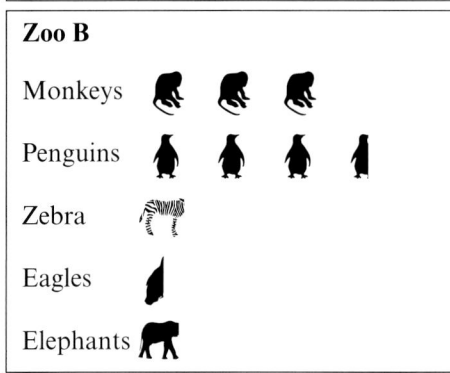

Zoo A
Monkeys
Penguins
Zebra
Eagles
Elephants
Zoo B
Monkeys
Penguins
Zebra
Eagles
Elephants

Key: 1 symbol = 5 animals

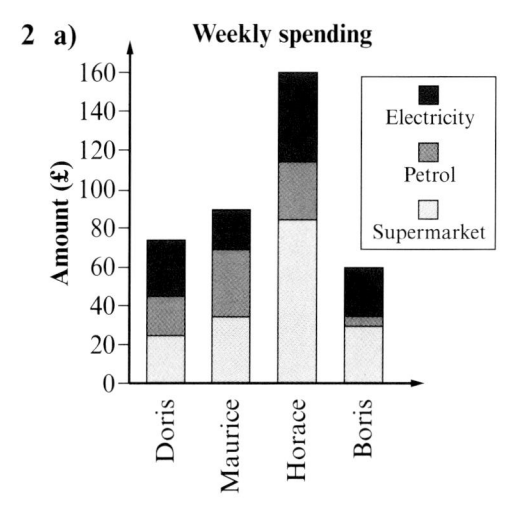

2 a)

Weekly spending
Amount (£)
160
140
120
100
80
60
40
20
0
Electricity
Petrol
Supermarket
Doris
Maurice
Horace
Boris

b) Horace is married with children.
c) Boris uses the train.

Review Exercise 19

1 Angles: tents 150°, rucksacks 90°, waterproofs 80°, maps 40°

2 Daily paper, angles: news 144°, advertising 126°, photos 90°
Sunday paper, angles: news 126°, advertising 180°, photos 54°

3 Angles: hockey 151°, cross-country 83°, squash 72°, swim 54°

4 **a)** There are 62 beads.
b) Red 134°, blue 93°, green 52°, yellow 81°
c) (Pie chart)

5 **a)**

Number of fillings	Tally	Frequency
0	~~IIII~~ ~~IIII~~	10
1	~~IIII~~ ~~IIII~~ IIII	14
2	IIII	4
3	II	2

b)

Dental fillings
Frequency
14
12
10
8
6
4
2
0
0
1
2
3
Number of fillings

6

Annabel
Henrietta
Daniel
David

1 symbol = 5 CDs

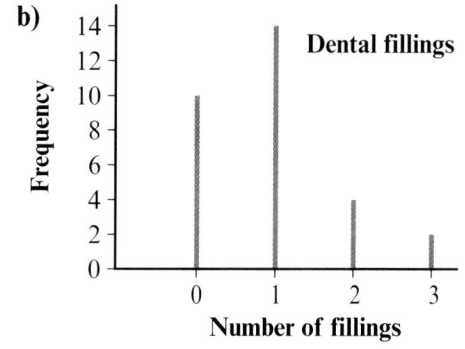

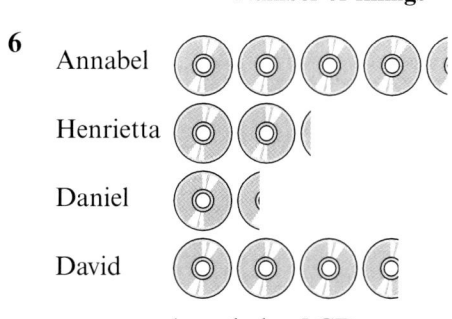

Level 5 Unit 19

7

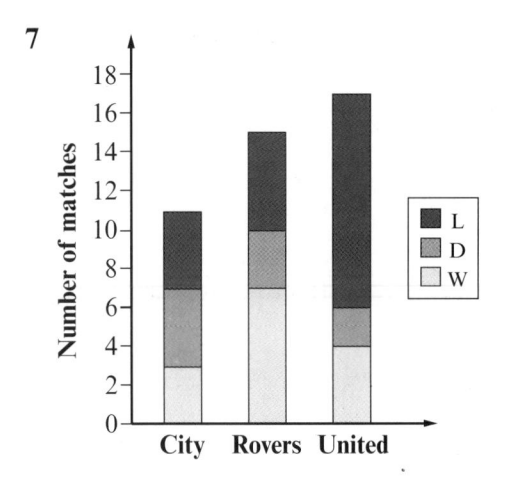

8 a) 160 acres
 b) 90°
 c) 480 acres

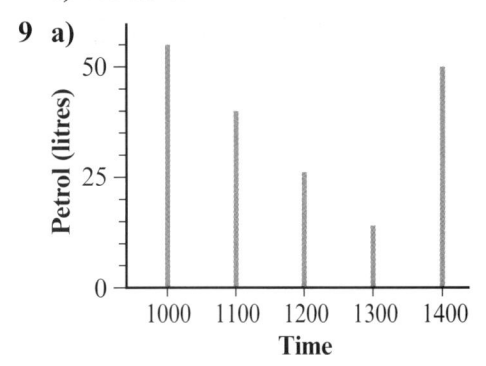

9 a)

 b) Joining the points up would be misleading because we don't really know at what time the car refuelled between 1300 and 1400.

10* a) Living room 130°, kitchen 70°, bathroom 55°, bedroom 80°, hall 25°.
 b) Sizes of rooms in a flat

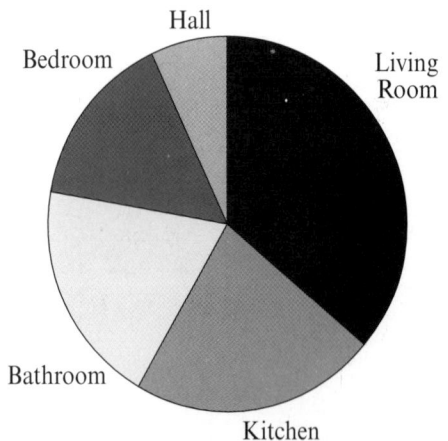

11 a) Mike   **b)** John
 c) 240 minutes (4 hours)

12 a) January 4
 b)

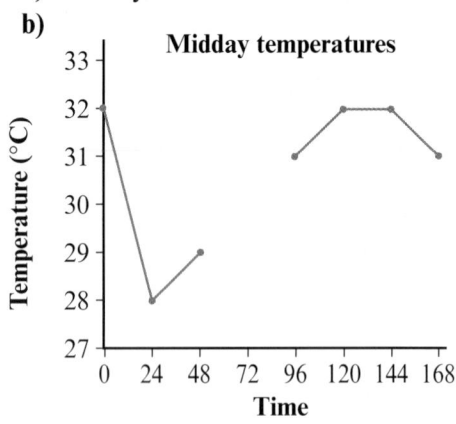

 The missing temperature is estimated as 30°C.
 c) Time 60 is actually midnight; it would be unwise to estimate this from the pattern of midday temperatures!

Unit 20
Theoretical and experimental probability

Exercise 20.1

This section builds on the work from Unit 10 by assigning a degree of likelihood to each outcome. At this stage verbal measures are still used, as a prelude to the numerical measures (on a scale of 0 to 1) used in the next section. The examples in Exercise 20.1 can be used, in discussion, to draw out the distinction between outcomes which are very unlikely (question 1) and impossible (question 3).

1. Unlikely
2. Very likely
3. Impossible
4. Unlikely
5. Reasonably likely
6. Certain
7. Unlikely
8. Very likely
9. Reasonably likely
10. Certain

Exercise 20.2

In this Unit answers should be given as fractions, cancelled as appropriate. The use of decimal approximation should be strongly discouraged.

1. a) $\frac{1}{2}$ b) $\frac{1}{13}$ c) $\frac{1}{52}$ d) $\frac{51}{52}$
2. a) $\frac{5}{18}$ b) $\frac{1}{3}$ c) 0
3. $\frac{1}{40}$
4. a) $\frac{1}{2}$ b) $\frac{3}{10}$ c) $\frac{4}{5}$ d) 0
5. $\frac{1}{3}$
6. a) $\frac{1}{2}$ b) $\frac{3}{13}$ c) $\frac{4}{13}$
7. a) $\frac{1}{2}$ b) $\frac{1}{6}$ c) $\frac{1}{3}$ d) $\frac{1}{3}$
8. a) $\frac{1}{2}$ b) $\frac{3}{20}$ c) $\frac{2}{5}$ d) $\frac{2}{5}$
9. a) $\frac{1}{5}$ b) $\frac{2}{5}$ c) $\frac{4}{5}$
   It is assumed that the company produces equal numbers of each type of toy aircraft.
10. a) $\frac{1}{2}$ b) $\frac{2}{5}$ c) $\frac{1}{5}$

Exercise 20.3

Once again, decimal approximations should be discouraged. While the arithmetic in the section is identical to that in the previous section, the emphasis is on understanding the difference between theoretical probability (a precise answer based on pure thought) and experimental probability (an imprecise answer, based on an experiment or the results of a survey etc.).

1. $\frac{7}{31}$
2. a) $\frac{19}{24}$ b) $\frac{5}{24}$
3. $\frac{13}{20}$
4. a) $\frac{11}{20}$ b) $\frac{9}{20}$
   They add up to 1, because they cover the only two possible results.
5. a) $\frac{1}{20}$ b) $\frac{2}{5}$

Review Exercise 20

1. $\frac{2}{5}$
2. $\frac{11}{14}$
3. $\frac{3}{10}$
4. $\frac{7}{50}$
5. $\frac{1}{52}$
6. $\frac{1}{2}$
7. $\frac{21}{26}$
8. $\frac{1}{5}$
9. $\frac{3}{10}$
10. $\frac{2}{3}$

11* a)

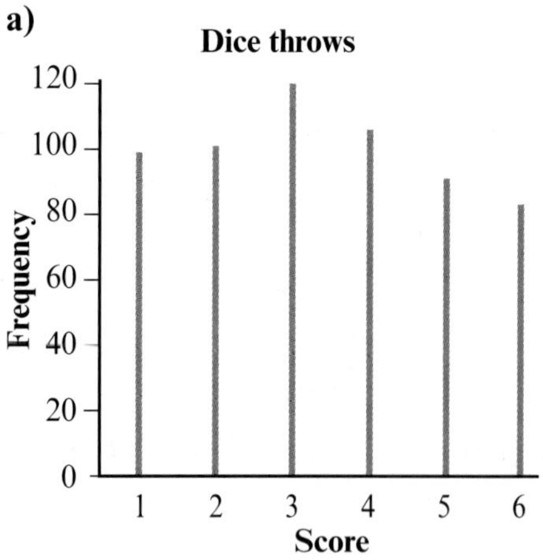
Dice throws
Frequency
120
100
80
60
40
20
0
1
2
3
4
5
6
Score

b) 0.17, 0.17, 0.2, 0.18, 0.15, 0.14

c) There seem to be too many threes and not enough sixes: the dice does not look fair.

12* 6 yellow, 9 blue, 9 purple

13* 32 (so that there are 40 balls in total)

14* a) $\frac{2}{15}$

b) Income so far 600p, paid out so far 400p, so the stall is expected to make money.

15* a) $\frac{33}{50}$ or 0.66

b) $\frac{149}{200}$ or 0.745

c) Emma's, because it uses more data.

d) Combine both sets of data (to obtain 0.728).

Level 5
Review

Exercise 1
1. 96
2. 9
3. 121
4. 7
5. 4 070 208
6. Two million, four hundred and six thousand, five hundred and forty-one
7. 788 000
8. 125
9. 4 625 000
10. 80 000
11. 50
12. 13 000
13. 4 000 000
14. 600 000
15. 26.3
16. 28.43
17. −2
18. 6
19. £30.24
20. 250

Exercise 2
1. 700 g
2. 8 sweets
3. £20
4. £60
5. 5800
6. 5p
7. 153 days
8. £168
9. $\frac{1}{13}$
10. $\frac{3}{20}$ (or 0.15)
11. 85
12. £8000
13. 225 pence each
14. £7.92
15. $\frac{1}{3}$
16. a) 90 cm   b) 30 fathoms
17. 4.5 litres
18. True
19. False – it should be 8 km and 5 miles
20. False – it should be 2500 g

Exercise 3
1. 7869
2. 6466
3. 17 538
4. 10 297
5. £43.51
6. £4.75
7. 4032
8. 170 234
9. 758
10. 449
11. 270
12. 400
13. 70 000 000 is probably only correct to 1 significant figure.
    70 000 001 to 1 s.f. is also 70 000 000
14. 87°, it is acute
15. 142°, it is obtuse
16. (180° − 118°) × 5 = 310°, not 360°. It should be 108°.
17. Mean 17.75, range 3, mode 19
18. 510°C
19. £30.47
20. 2.85 m

Exercise 4
1. 119
2. 598
3. $19a − 11b$
4. $18x^2$
5. £13.52
6. 72.5
7. a) 40   b) 8
8. John, by £4 a month
9. 35
10. $14b − 2a$, −32.2
11. £100 − 5n, n cannot exceed 20
12. 217.2 people
13. a)

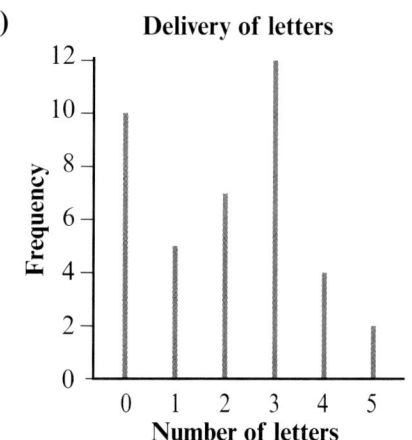

    Delivery of letters

    (bar chart: Frequency vs Number of letters; 0→10, 1→5, 2→7, 3→12, 4→4, 5→2)

    b) The mode is 3 letters
    c) $n = 40$, $\frac{15}{40}$ (or $\frac{3}{8}$ or 0.375)
14. a) Mean 19.33
    b) Mode 19, range 6

Level 5 Review

15 a) 65
  b) $6 \times 55 - 5 \times 51 = 75$ marks needed, but the maximum mark is only 70.

16 a) 43   **b)** 47   **c)** 1763
  d) 1763 is not prime (it is 41×43)

17 b) 35% is left over; it is equivalent to $\frac{7}{20}$.
  $\frac{4}{5}$ is left over; it is equivalent to 80%.

18 1 is about 10 times too small. ($2000 \times 200 = 400\,000$) John missed out the first zero, in 401 064.
  2 is correct. ($30 \times 90 = 2700$)
  3 is correct. ($10\,000 \div 100 = 100$)

19 a) A time series graph is better, as time is continuous
  b)

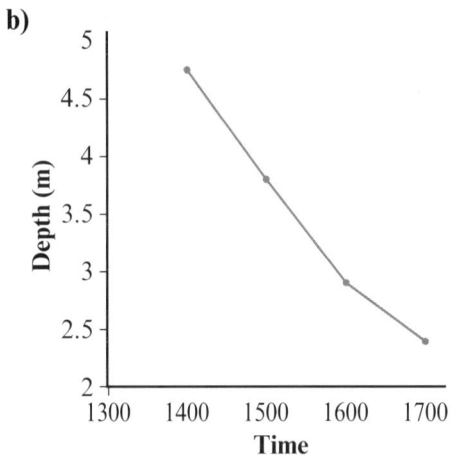

At 1630 the depth is about 2.6 m (or 2.7)

20 a) Angles: soaps and sitcoms 126°, sports 97°, news 65°, other 72°.

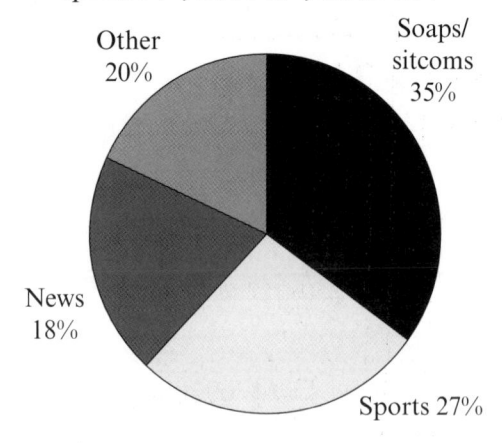

  b) 97°
  c) 720 people

Exercise 5

	¹S	H	²E	L	³L		⁴E	E	⁵L
	O		G		⁶I	L	L		E
	⁷L	E	G	⁸S			⁹L	¹⁰O	G
	E			¹¹S	O	L	¹²O		B
			¹³L		I		I		E
			E		¹⁴L	I	L	¹⁵O		¹⁶H
	¹⁷H	O	¹⁸E				¹⁹S	H	O	E
	O		²⁰B	E	²¹E		I		B
	²²B	O	B		²³L	O	O	S	E

44

Level 6 Unit 21
Rounding and approximation

Exercise 21.1

In this section the two main skills practised are rounding (either to a given number of significant figures or decimal places) and ordering lists of positive decimals.
The last question in the exercise includes some negative numbers; some pupils may need reminding that the smallest numbers are those furthest to the left along a directed number line, so −2 is smaller than −1, for example.

1	13.6	2	104.8
3	3.07	4	88.222
5	16.46	6	12.20
7	3.142	8	60.3
9	17.3	10	46.20
11	14.2	12	0.00203

13 6.21, 6.065, 4.601, 4.3, 4.03
14 12.901, 12.66, 12.2, 12.109, 12.01
15 4.21, 4.201, 4.021, 1.24, 1.024
16 0.2, 0.03, 0.02, 0.010, 0.001
17 1.402, 1.61, 10.42, 14.02, 14.2
18 30.63, 33.13, 33.6, 36.03, 36.3
19 4.07, 4.17, 4.7, 4.81, 4.87
20 −3.6, −2.14, −1.44, 0.26, 0.77

Exercise 21.2

It is worth emphasising that a KS3 or GCSE examiner will expect to see all the trials written down as well as the final answer.
A spreadsheet such as Excel offers an opportunity to perform trial and improvement work without the tedium of large numbers of calculator key strokes, but should only be considered once the basic idea has been well understood.

1	1.54	2	8.11	3	2.791	4	0.85
5	3.70	6	1.59	7	6.41	8	7.04
9	1.5	10	0.19				

Exercise 21.3

These problems can all be done by calculator or, as suggested in the text, using a spreadsheet. Either way, it is good style to rearrange the equation first so that the right hand side is zero.
The phrase 'a positive solution' might need to be explained; questions 1, 2 and 4 actually possess two positive solutions so the answers to these are not unique.

1	2.6 (or 0.4)	2	1.9 (or 0.3)
3	2.7	4	3.1 (or 0.6)
5	1.4	6	2.7
7	1.4	8	7.3
9	3.07 and 0.90	10	0.773

Review Exercise 21

1 a) 44.221   b) 6.67   c) 0.0003
   d) 8.4250   e) 3.818 f) 2.00
2 a) 83.21   b) 410   c) 319.0
   d) 452 000 e) 0.00036 f) 1200
   g) 1.00   h) 12.00   i) 1
3 Consider $x^3 - x - 64$
   When $x = 4$ this is −4, i.e. negative
   When $x = 5$ this is 56, i.e. positive.
   Therefore a solution lies between 4 and 5.
   Trial and improvement gives $x = 4.08$

45

Level 6 Unit 21

4* a) They can both be right because the equation could have two (or more) solutions.
   b) 0.41 and −2.41 ($x = 1$ is also a solution)

5* a) 5.24 **b)** −3.2

6* a) Tim and Natalie are right.
   b) 4.49 and 7.59 (each to 2 d.p.)

7* a) −3, 4, 3, 0 and 1, $a = 3$
   b) 3.73
   c) c lies between 0 and 1, $c = 0.27$

Unit 22
Number patterns

Exercise 22.1

In order to develop algebraic rules later in the Unit it is important to encourage precision with the descriptions in words. 'It goes up 3 at a time' is too vague; whereas 'the pattern starts at 4 and goes up 3 at a time' is acceptable.

1. Starts at 5, goes up 2 at a time; 15, 17.
2. Starts at 11, goes up 5 at a time; 36, 41.
3. Starts at 16, goes up 3 at a time; 31, 34.
4. Starts at 11, goes down 2 at a time; 1, –1.
5. Starts at 40, goes down 4 at a time: 20, 16.
6. Starts at 1, doubles each time; 32, 64.
7. Starts at 1, goes up 2, then 3, etc; 21, 28.
8. Starts at 45, goes up 9 at a time; 90, 99.
9. Starts at 11, goes up 11 at a time; 66, 77.
10. Starts at 100, goes down 1, then 2, etc; 85, 79.

Exercise 22.2

It is important to distinguish between a term-to-term rule (which only explains how adjacent terms are connected) and a position-to-term rule. It may be said that a position-to-term rule is more powerful: the 100th term of a pattern can be found directly using a position-to-term rule, whereas all the intervening terms need to be computed as well if a term-to-term rule is used.

1. 5, 7, 9, 11, 13
2. 14, 19, 24, 29, 34
3. 2, 6, 10, 14, 18
4. 1, 4, 7, 10, 13
5. 101, 102, 103, 104, 105
6. 8, 6, 4, 2, 0
7. 31, 32, 33, 34, 35
8. 30, 40, 50, 60, 70
9. 0, 2, 6, 12, 20
10. 1, 4, 9, 16, 25
11. 1, 2, 4, 8, 16, 32
12. 1, 3, 7, 15, 31, 63
13. 3, 7, 19, 55, 163, 487
14. 4, 6, 12, 30, 84, 246
15. 3, 3, 3, 3, 3, 3
16. 4, 6, 4, 6, 4, 6
17. 4, –6, –16, –26, –36, –46
18. 1, 2, 4, 7, 11, 16
19. 32, 64, 128, 256, 512, 1024
20. 32, 16, 8, 4, 2, 1

Exercise 22.3

The ability to write down a position-to-term rule for a linear pattern is a recurring theme in GCSE coursework tasks.
It might be worth doing a practice task, employing the method of differences, as a way of concluding and consolidating this whole topic.

Level 6 Unit 22

1. 21, 23; $u_n = 2n + 9$
2. 25, 28; $u_n = 3n + 7$
3. 11, 12; $u_n = n + 5$
4. 35, 40; $u_n = 5n + 5$
5. 25, 20; $u_n = 55 - 5n$
6. 20, 22; $u_n = 2n + 8$
7. 35, 38; $u_n = 3n + 17$
8. −5, −8; $u_n = 13 - 3n$
9. 39, 46; $u_n = 7n - 3$
10. 45, 34; $u_n = 111 - 11n$
11. Linear; $u_n = 2n + 19$
12. Not linear; goes up by 2, then 3, then 4 etc.
13. Linear; $u_n = 3n + 18$
14. Not linear; goes up by 3, then 5, then 7 etc.
15. Not linear; terms are doubled each time.
16. Linear; $u_n = 11 - 3n$
17. Linear; $u_n = 10n - 2$
18. Not linear; the pattern is actually a list of prime numbers.
19. Linear; $u_n = 20n + 40$
20. Not linear; the pattern is actually a list of perfect cubes.

Review Exercise 22

1. 122, 116, 111, 107, 104, 102, 101, 101
2. 7, 12, 17, 22, 27, 32, 37, 42
3. 13, 14, 16, 19, 23, 28, 34, 41
4. 22, 20, 18, 16, 14, 12, 10, 8
5. Position-to-term; 0, 3, 6, 9, 12, 15
6. Term-to-term; 1, 4, 7, 10, 13, 16
7. Position-to-term; 2, 5, 10, 17, 26, 37
8. Position-to-term; −6, −1, 4, 9, 14, 19
9. Position-to-term; 3, 7, 13, 21, 31, 43
10. Term-to-term; 1, 3, 9, 27, 81, 243
11. Position-to-term; 20, 22, 24, 26, 28, 30
12. Term-to-term; 20, 62, 188, 566, 1700, 5102
13. Linear; $u_n = 3n + 57$
14. Not linear; $u_1 = 10$ and $u_{n+1} = 3u_n$
15. Not linear; $u_1 = 80$ and $u_{n+1} = 0.5 \times u_n$
16. Linear; $u_n = 10n - 17$
17. Not linear; $u_1 = 1$ and $u_{n+1} = 5u_n$
18. Linear; $u_n = 10 - 2n$
19. Linear; $u_n = 6n + 4$
20. Not linear; $u_1 = 243$ and $u_{n+1} = u_n \div 3$
21*. a) 40, 70, 100, 130, 160, 190
    b) $30n + 10$ c) $0.3n + 0.1$
22*. a) 1, 3, 5, 7, 9
    b) The first five (positive) odd numbers
    c) (i) Even numbers, starting at 2
       (ii) Positive whole numbers, starting at 1
       (iii) Triangular numbers
23*. a) 8, 14, 20, 26, 32
    b) $u_{n+1} = u_n + 6$
    c) $u_n = 6n + 2$
24*. a) $u_n = 42n + 33\,534$;
       Then $u_{11} = 42 \times 11 + 33\,534$
           $= 33\,996$
    b) In reality u_{11} would only have a meaning if the journey continued uninterrupted for $5\frac{1}{2}$ hours, which is not very likely!
25*. a) 1, 1, 2, 3, 5, 8, 13, 21, 34, 55
    b) 0.618 and 0.618; they are the same (to 3 d.p.)
    c) 89, 144, 233, 377, 610; this gives 0.618 again
    d) Leonardo of Pisa is better known as Fibonacci. This number pattern is called a Fibonacci sequence. The ratio 0.618 is used in golden ratio constructions in many famous buildings and paintings.

Unit 23
Fractions, decimals and percentages

Teachers may wish to consider a different teaching order from that presented here.

Exercise 23.1

Watch for incomplete cancelling, e.g. $\frac{42}{78}$ cancelled to $\frac{21}{39}$ but not taken any further. Watch also for errors arising in questions with units.

1. a) $\frac{14}{19}$ b) $\frac{4}{7}$ c) $\frac{19}{24}$ d) $\frac{3}{7}$
   e) $\frac{7}{19}$ f) $\frac{21}{41}$ g) $\frac{7}{45}$ h) $\frac{5}{24}$
   i) $\frac{13}{38}$ j) $\frac{1}{2}$

2. a) 80% b) 76% c) 15%
   d) 40% e) 70% f) $17\frac{1}{2}$%
   g) 37% h) 30% i) 17%
   j) 30%

Exercise 23.2

Mixed fraction problems can be dealt with in several equivalent ways. Beware of encouraging, e.g. 3.725 as $\frac{3275}{1000}$ then cancelling down, as this can lead to quite heavy arithmetic; the illustrated method of truncating the whole number part first is superior in this respect.

1. a) 0.375 b) 2.7 c) 5.25
   d) 0.2727 e) 2.3333 f) 0.4444
   g) 0.4167 h) 3.1429 i) 0.4375
   j) 4.6429

2. a) $\frac{22}{25}$ b) $\frac{31}{250}$ c) $\frac{9}{40}$
   d) $4\frac{3}{20}$ e) $3\frac{16}{25}$ f) $\frac{9}{250}$
   g) $2\frac{19}{20}$ h) $\frac{33}{50}$ i) $1\frac{17}{20}$
   j) $\frac{79}{250}$

Exercise 23.3

Few difficulties should be encountered, other than with fractional percentages such as 2b $33\frac{1}{3}$%.

1. a) 38% b) 70% c) 31.5%
   d) 20.5% e) 143% f) 620%
   g) 170.7% h) 8% i) 10%
   j) 440%

2. a) 0.65 b) $0.\dot{3}$ c) 0.025
   d) 0.18 e) 1.5 f) 0.77
   g) 0.06 h) 0.075 i) 1.05
   j) 0.88

Exercise 23.4

Encourage the use of multiplying factors rather than apparently simpler alternative methods. The multiplying factor comes into its own in reverse problems, such as question 5.

1. a) 28 250 b) 371 c) 6150
   d) $231 e) £936
2. a) 1.15 b) 30 200
3. a) 0.89 b) £34.71
4. a) 1.175 b) £821.33
5. a) 1.12 b) £18.50
6. 375 g

Level 6 Unit 23

Exercise 23.5

Some pupils can find ratio surprisingly difficult, and will need many more practice questions. The use of a calculator fraction key is an effective way of simplifying a straightforward ratio, but fails with a triple ratio such as 100:65:55.

1. a) 4:7 b) 3:4 c) 5:4
    d) 5:7 e) 7:11 f) 5:9
    g) 8:12:15 h) 20:13:11 i) 3:6:7
    j) 7:18:13 k) 7:48 l) 9:70
2. 3:5 (or 5:3)
3. a) 3:5:12 b) 45 min
4. a) 3:5:4
    b) 48 cassettes
    c) 20 are jazz

Review Exercise 23

1. a) $\frac{2}{5}$, 40% b) $\frac{11}{20}$, 55%
    c) $\frac{5}{8}$, 62.5% d) $\frac{3}{5}$, 60%
    e) $\frac{1}{5}$, 20% f) $\frac{23}{400}$, 5.75%
    g) $\frac{13}{20}$, 65% h) $\frac{9}{10}$, 90%
2. a) 0.85 b) 0.625
    c) 0.714 d) 4.7
    e) 0.889 f) 3.333
    g) 0.74 h) 2.07
3. a) $\frac{3}{50}$, 6% b) $\frac{13}{20}$, 65%
    c) $\frac{7}{25}$, 28% d) $\frac{11}{25}$, 44%
    e) $\frac{1}{40}$, 2.5% f) $\frac{1}{8}$, 12.5%
    g) $2\frac{3}{5}$, 260% h) $1\frac{2}{25}$, 108%
4. a) 0.25 b) 0.09
    c) 0.225 d) 2.04
5. Lois gets £9.75 and Richard gets £5.25
6. a) 5:2:3
    b) 100 silver birch, 40 maple and 60 oak
7. a) 7800 b) 10140 c) 28961
8. Including VAT, *Bargain PC Supplies* costs £175.08, so *Bargain PC* is the cheaper overall.
9. a) 20% are red.
    b) 16 red, 20 green, 44 yellow
10. 2:5:7
11.* 1:10:100
12.* a) 3:4 b) 9:16
13.* $110
14.* 70 mm
15.* a) 1.12 b) 1.2
    c) 1.12 × 1.2 = 1.344 so his increase is 34.4%, not 32%
16.* a) 3:25 b) 750 francs
    c) 1:10 d) 900 francs
    e) 20% (because 900 ÷ 750 = 1.20)

Unit 24
Linear equations

Exercise 24.1

This first section looks at one-step solutions involving the reverse of addition, subtraction, multiplication or division. The reverse processes should be explicitly stated, in preparation for harder questions later; it is unproductive for pupils to use trial and improvement or inspection instead.

1 $x = 15$	**2** $x = 17$	**3** $x = -7$
4 $x = 32$	**5** $x = 16$	**6** $x = -1$
7 $x = 8$	**8** $x = 7$	**9** $x = 5.5$
10 $x = 27$	**11** $x = 33$	**12** $x = 78$
13 $x = 23$	**14** $x = 5$	**15** $x = 91$
16 $x = 3$	**17** $x = -1$	**18** $x = 18$
19 $x = 12$	**20** $x = 5$	

Exercise 24.2

Once again, inspection is to be discouraged. The idea is to apply one initial step, after which the equation should resemble those solved in the previous section.

1 $x = 6$	**2** $x = 9$	**3** $x = 7$
4 $x = 3$	**5** $x = 3$	**6** $x = 6$
7 $x = 12$	**8** $x = 6$	**9** $x = 3$
10 $x = 12$	**11** $x = 4$	**12** $x = 7$
13 $x = 6$	**14** $x = -4$	**15** $x = 1.5$
16 $x = 5$	**17** $x = 4$	**18** $x = 2.5$
19 $x = 2.5$	**20** $x = 8$	

Exercise 24.3

The secret of success here is to be patient; proceed one small step at a time. Pupils should be encouraged to write solutions out in full, with the = signs aligned, as in the examples on pages 173 and 174.

1 $x = 2$ **2** $x = 8$ **3** $x = 8$
4 $x = 3$ **5** $x = 7$ **6** $x = -3$
7 $x = 7$ **8** $x = 0$ **9** $x = 3$
10 $x = 4$ **11** $x = 4.5$
12 $x = 4\frac{2}{3}$ (or 4.667)
13 $x = -2\frac{1}{3}$ (or -2.333)
14 $x = 3\frac{3}{5}$ (or 3.6)
15 $x = 3\frac{1}{4}$ (or 3.25)
16 $x = 6\frac{4}{5}$ (or 6.8)
17 $x = 2\frac{3}{4}$ (or 2.75)
18 $x = 5$
19 $x = -2\frac{3}{5}$ (or -2.6)
20 $x = -1\frac{2}{5}$ (or -1.4)

Exercise 24.4

The Unit finishes with some problems in context. The unknown number (dogs, Tim's age or whatever) is represented by x, and the words are then transformed into an equation. It is important to write the equation accurately in its original form first; only then should the process of solving begin.

1 $3x + 11 = 59$; $x = 16$;
The number was 16.

Level 6 Unit 24

2 $4x + 18 = 70$; $x = 13$; The rectangle is 13 cm by 22 cm.

3 $4x = x + 84$; $x = 28$; She has 28 dogs.

4 $6x + 7 = 61$; $x = 9$; I thought of 9.

5 $10x - 43 = 5x + 7$; $x = 10$; Tim and Gavin are each 10 years old.

6 $7x + 4 = 100 - x$; $x = 12$; Flora's number was 12.

10* a) $7x + 17 = 5x + 55$
   b) $x = 19$, so a pencil costs 19 pence.

11* a) $7x - 7 = 61 + 5x$
   then $x = 34$
   b) AB = 231, AC = 231, BC = 118
   c) The perimeter is 580 units.

Review Exercise 24

1 a) $x = 28$ **b)** $x = 13$
  c) $x = 8$ **d)** $x = -5$
  e) $x = 32$ **f)** $x = 68$
  g) $x = 11$ **h)** $x = 33$

2 a) $x = 8$ **b)** $x = 9$
  c) $x = 2$ **d)** $x = 11$
  e) $x = -4$ **f)** $x = -5$
  g) $x = 9\frac{1}{4}$ (or 9.25)
  h) $x = 5\frac{1}{2}$ (or 5.5)

3 a) $x = 4$ **b)** $x = -2$
  c) $x = 6$ **d)** $x = 5$
  e) $x = 5$ **f)** $x = 8$

4 a) $3x + 4 = 28 - x$
  b) $x = 6$, so the perimeter of the square is $4 \times 22 = 88$ cm.

5 a) $7x + 13 = 69$
  b) $x = 8$

6 a) $n + 2$ **b)** $2n$
  c) $4n + 2 = 62$, and so $n = 15$
  d) 15 red, 17 blue, 30 yellow

7* 35 (he thought of the number 9)

8* a) $x = 8$
  b) 75 mm

9* a) $3x - 100 = x + 34$
  b) $x = 67$, so grandma is 67 years old.

Unit 25
Functions and graphs

Exercise 25.1

Few difficulties are likely to be encountered with mapping diagrams, though it is important to encourage accurate use of vocabulary. Lines should be marked with arrows showing the direction of the mapping.

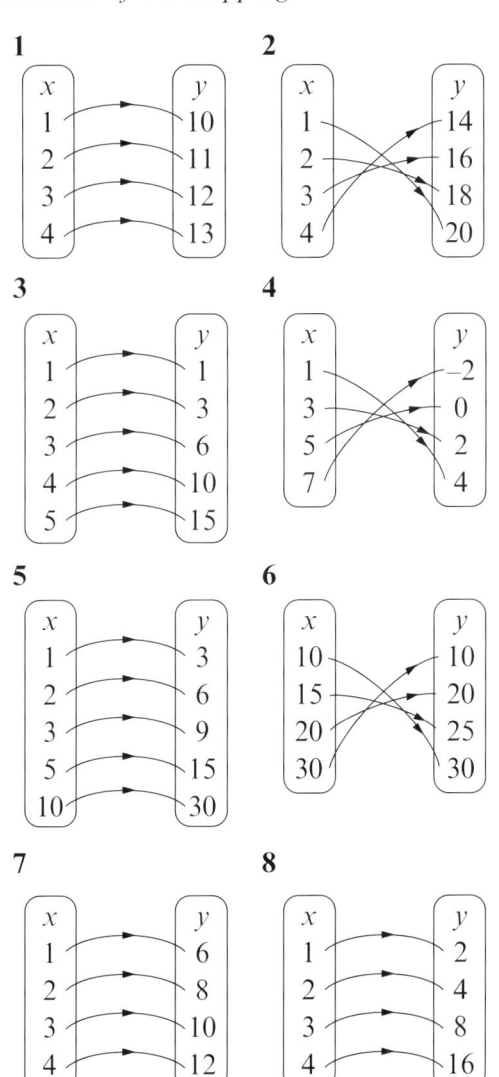

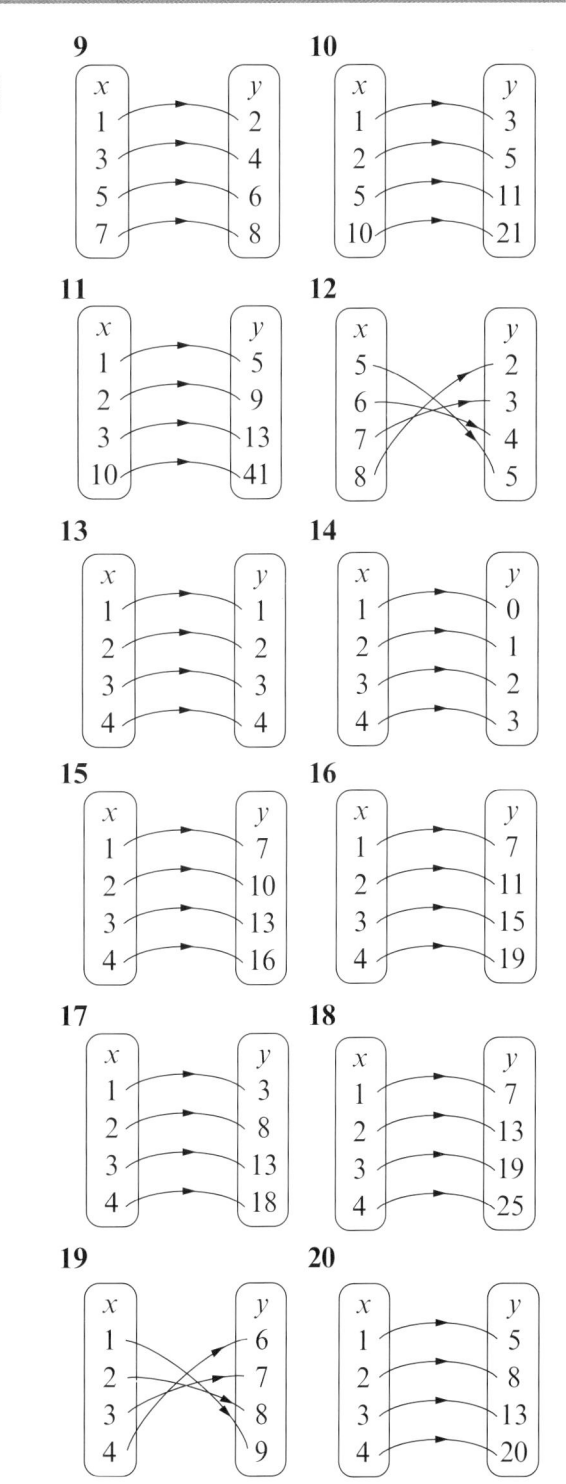

1

x	y
1 →	10
2 →	11
3 →	12
4 →	13

2

x	y
1	14
2	16
3	18
4	20

3

x	y
1 →	1
2 →	3
3 →	6
4 →	10
5 →	15

4

x	y
1	−2
3	0
5	2
7	4

5

x	y
1 →	3
2 →	6
3 →	9
5 →	15
10 →	30

6

x	y
10	10
15	20
20	25
30	30

7

x	y
1 →	6
2 →	8
3 →	10
4 →	12

8

x	y
1 →	2
2 →	4
3 →	8
4 →	16

9

x	y
1 →	2
3 →	4
5 →	6
7 →	8

10

x	y
1 →	3
2 →	5
5 →	11
10 →	21

11

x	y
1 →	5
2 →	9
3 →	13
10 →	41

12

x	y
5	2
6	3
7	4
8	5

13

x	y
1 →	1
2 →	2
3 →	3
4 →	4

14

x	y
1 →	0
2 →	1
3 →	2
4 →	3

15

x	y
1 →	7
2 →	10
3 →	13
4 →	16

16

x	y
1 →	7
2 →	11
3 →	15
4 →	19

17

x	y
1 →	3
2 →	8
3 →	13
4 →	18

18

x	y
1 →	7
2 →	13
3 →	19
4 →	25

19

x	y
1	6
2	7
3	8
4	9

20

x	y
1 →	5
2 →	8
3 →	13
4 →	20

Exercise **25.2**

Two points are sufficient to define a line; the purpose of the third is as a check. The points should be chosen to be as far apart as possible, so that the line may be drawn with maximum accuracy.

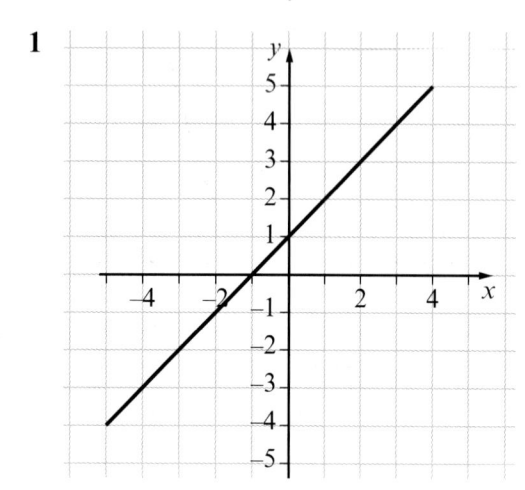

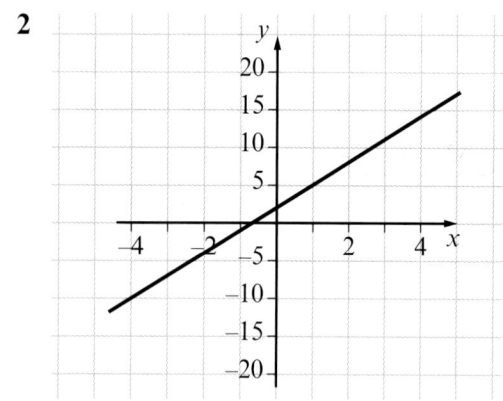

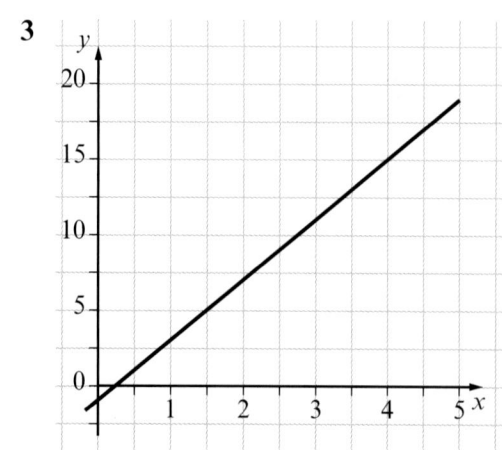

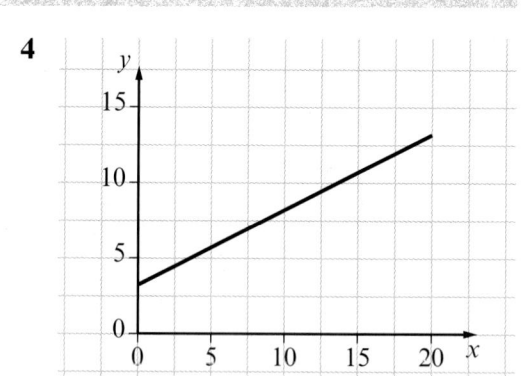

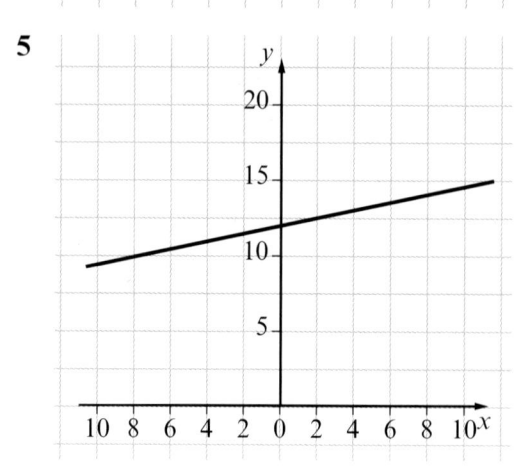

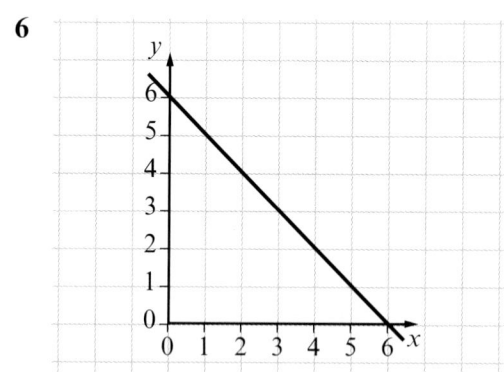

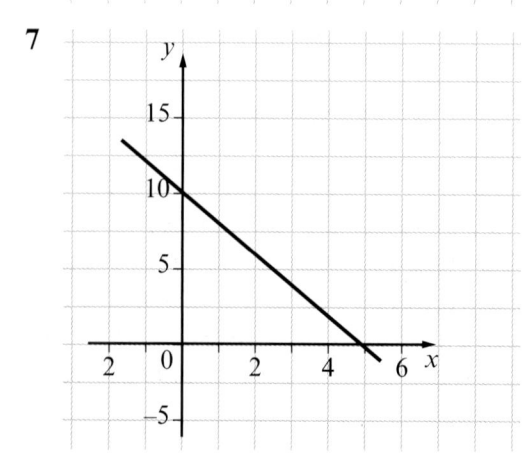

Level 6 Unit 25

8

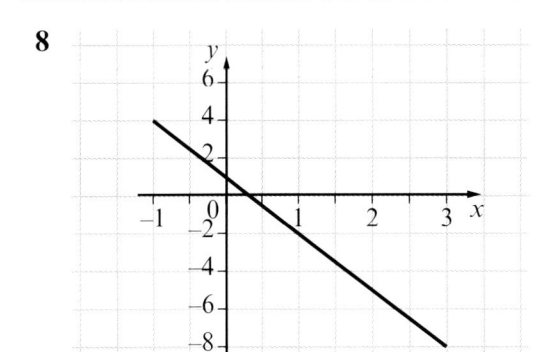

9

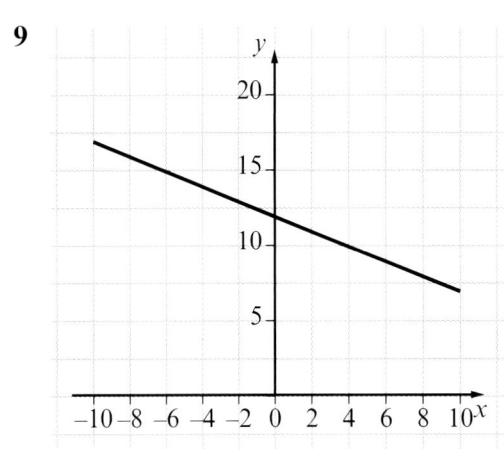

10

1

x	−4	−3	−2	−1	0	1	2	3
x^2	16	9	4	1	0	1	4	9
+4x	−16	−12	−8	−4	0	4	8	12
−3	−3	−3	−3	−3	−3	−3	−3	−3
y	−3	−6	−7	−6	−3	2	9	18

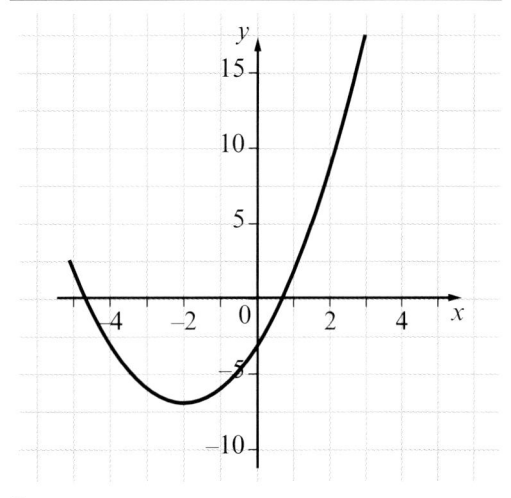

2

x	−3	−2	−1	0	1	2	3
10	10	10	10	10	10	10	10
+2x	−6	−4	−2	−0	2	4	6
$-x^2$	−9	−4	−1	0	−1	−4	−9
y	−5	2	7	10	11	10	7

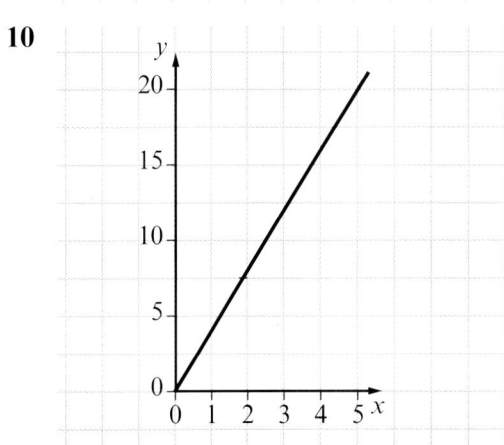

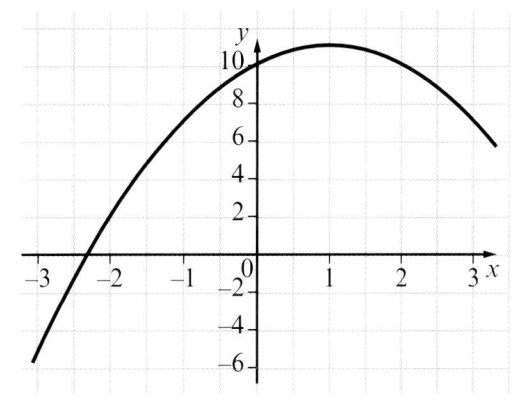

Exercise 25.3

Graph plotting software such as Omnigraph or Autograph can be useful in checking results here, but should not be introduced before the basic idea of how to plot a graph by hand has been mastered.

Level 6 Unit 25

3

x	−2	−1	0	1	2	3	4
$2x^2$	8	2	0	2	8	18	32
$-4x$	8	4	0	−4	−8	−12	−16
−1	−1	−1	−1	−1	−1	−1	−1
y	15	5	−1	−3	−1	5	15

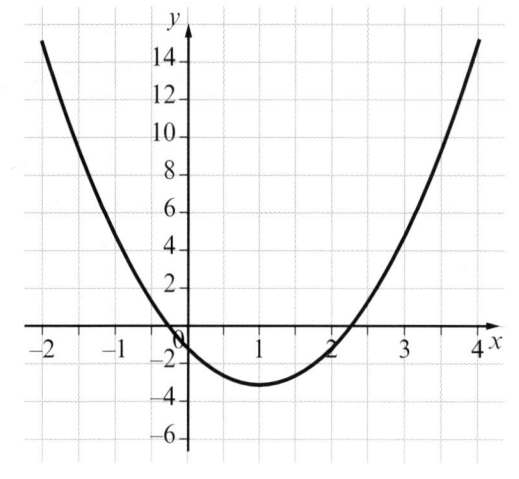

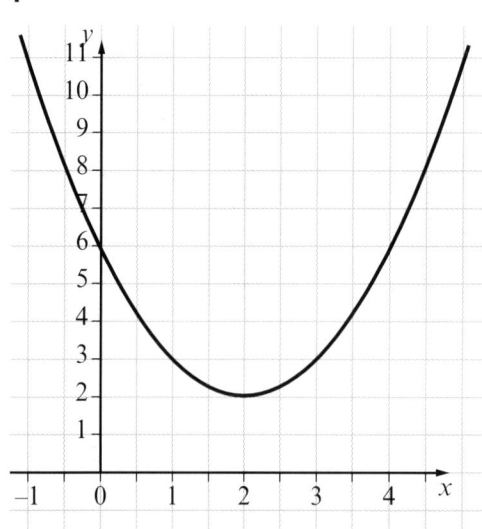

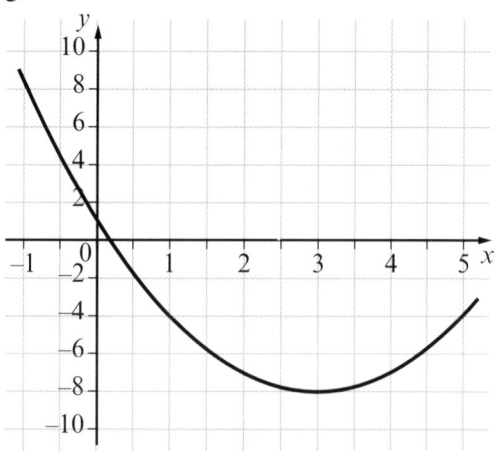

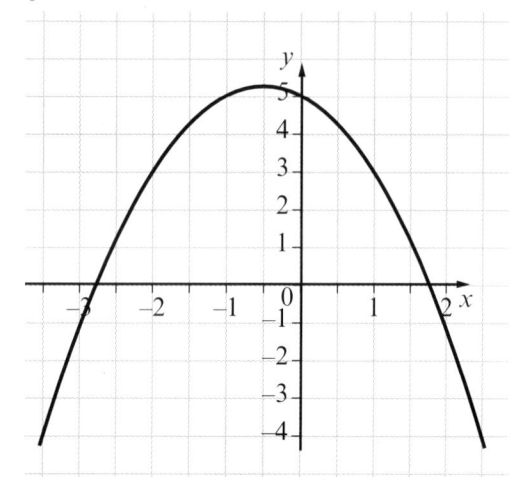

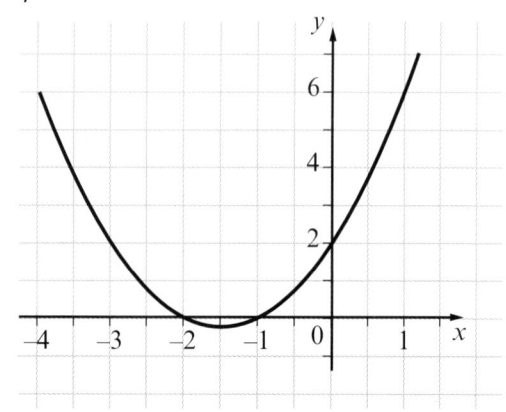

4

5

6

7

Level 6 Unit 25

8

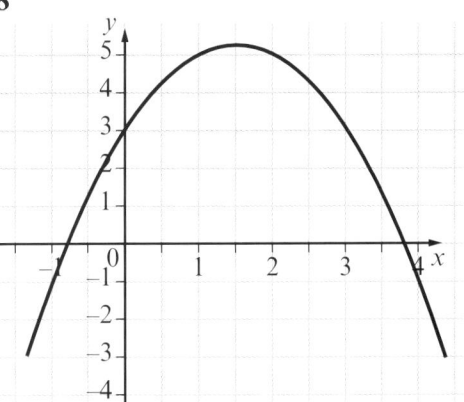

9

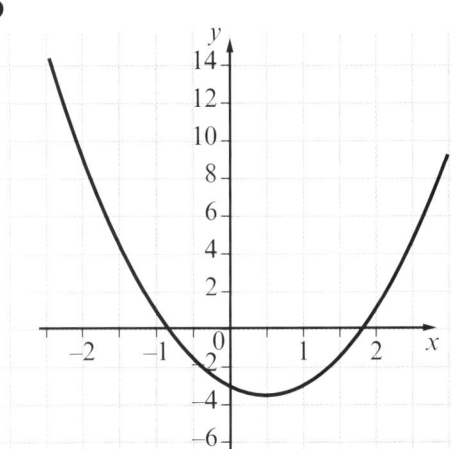

10

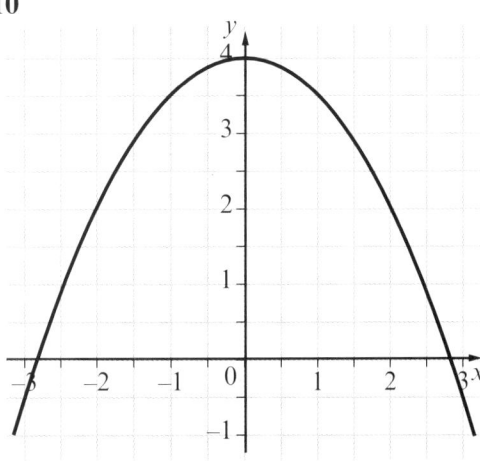

Review Exercise 25

1

a)
x	y
–1 →	1
0 →	2
1 →	3
2 →	4
3 →	5

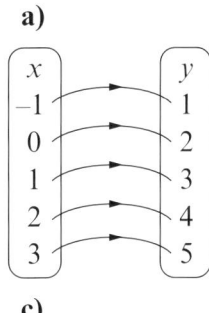

b)
x	y
–1 →	1
0 →	3
1 →	5
2 →	7
3 →	9

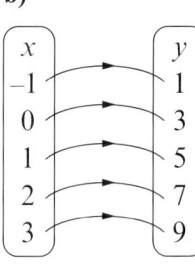

c)
x	y
–1	–1
0	0
1	1
2	2
3	3

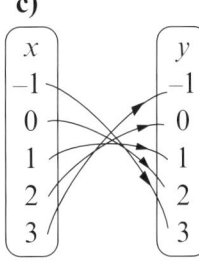

d)
x	y
–1 →	0
0 →	–1
1 →	0
2 →	3
3 →	8

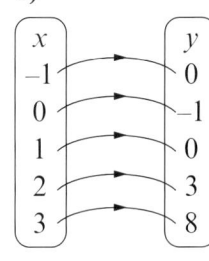

2 a) The missing number is 11.
Add 1 to each x value. $y = x + 1$

b) The missing number is 6.
Multiply each x value by 3. $y = 3x$

c) The missing number is 13.
Multiply each x value by 4, then add 1. $y = 4x + 1$

d) The missing number is 4.
Multiply each x value by 2, then subtract 1. $y = 2x - 1$

3 a)
x	–3	0	2	5
y	–9	–3	1	7

b)

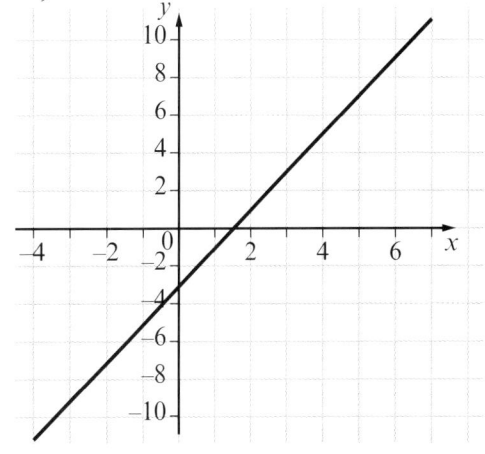

57

Level 6 Unit 25

4 a)

x	−1	0	2	4
y	8	5	−1	−7

b)

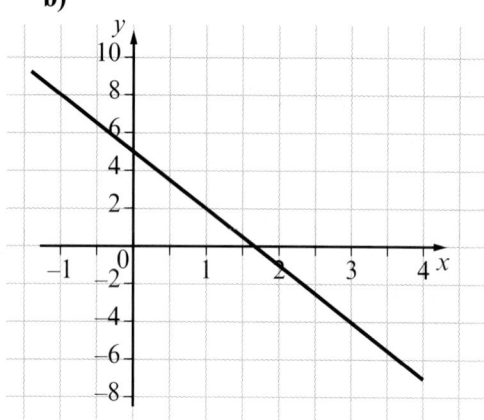

5

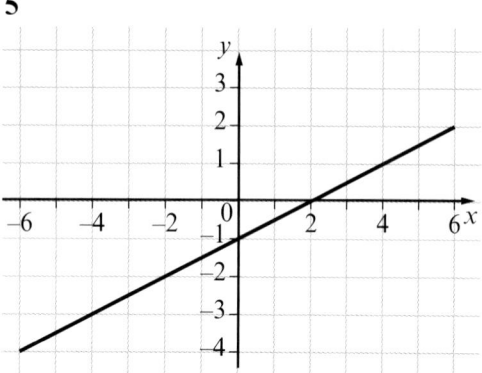

6

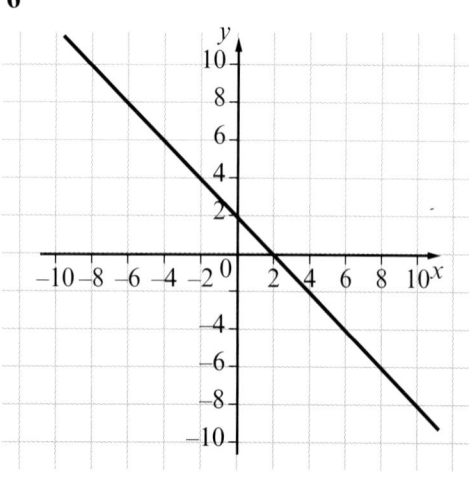

7

a)

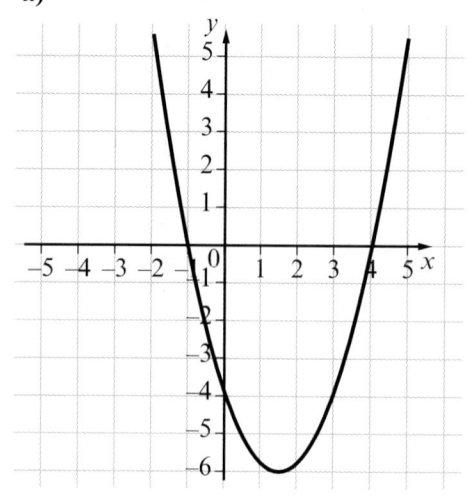

b)

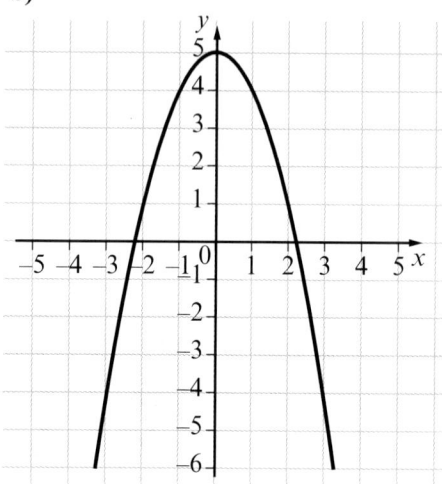

c)

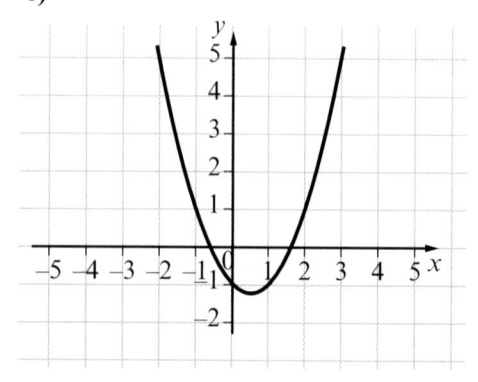

d)

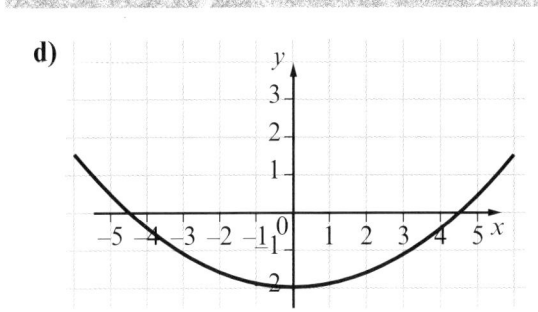

8* a) and **b)**

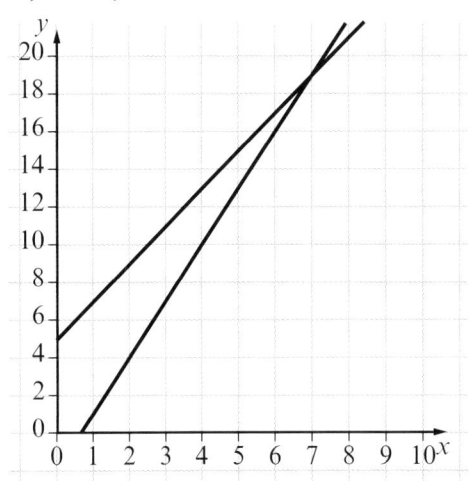

c) The lines cross at (7, 19)

9* a) D **b)** A **c)** B **d)** C

10* a) D **b)** A **c)** B **d)** C

11* a)

x	0	1	2	3	4	5	6
y	10	12	12	10	6	0	−8

b) Maximum height is 12.25.

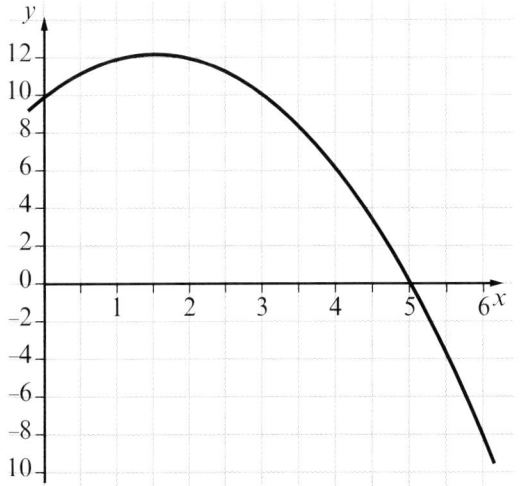

c) The ball lands at time 5.

Unit 26
Quadrilaterals and angles

Exercise 26.1

Some revision of coordinates might be useful before starting this section.

1. This is a parallelogram.

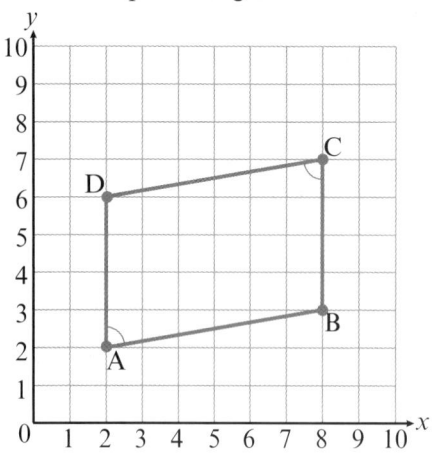

2. This is a rhombus.

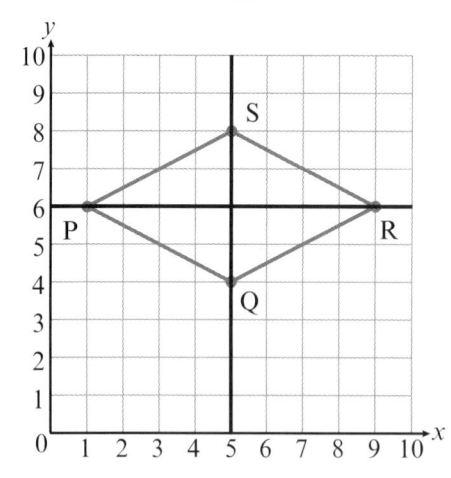

3. This is a square.
4. This is a trapezium.
5. This is a rectangle. X is at $(5\frac{1}{2}, 5)$
6. This is a parallelogram. It has no line of symmetry.
7. This is a square. It has rotational symmetry of order 4.
8. This is an isosceles trapezium. It has one line of symmetry.
9. This quadrilateral has no special name. It has no line of symmetry.
10. A parallelogram 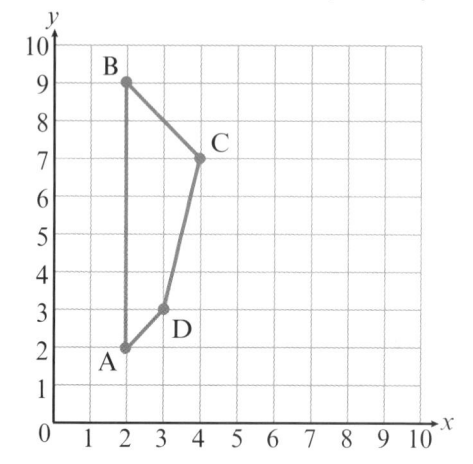

Exercise 26.2

Reasons may be kept very brief, and may use either traditional (corresponding angles) or modern (F-angles) vocabulary. If several angles are to be found in the same diagram, examiners often label them in alphabetical order, e.g. find s first, then t, then u.

1. $a = 92°$ (angles in a quadrilateral)
2. $b = 93°$ (angles on a straight line)
   $c = 113°$ (angles in a quadrilateral)
   $d = 67°$ (angles on a straight line)

Level 6 Unit 26

3 $e = 100°$ (angles on a straight line)
    $f = 100°$ (symmetry of a kite)

4 $g = 108°$ (angles on a straight line)

5 $h = 60°$ (angles on a straight line)

6 $i = 120°$ (angles at a point)

7 $j = 149°$ (angles on a straight line)

8 $k = 110°$ (angles at a point)

9 $l = 35°$ (vertically opposite)
    $m = 145°$ (angles on a straight line)
    $n = 145°$ (vertically opposite)

10 $p = 42°$ (Z-angles)

11 $q = 125°$ (angles on a straight line)
     $r = 125°$ (interior angles)

12 $s = 90°$ (angles on a straight line)
     $t = 60°$ (Z-angles)
     $u = 30°$ (Z-angles)

13 $v = 105°$ (vertically opposite)
     $w = 75°$ (interior angles)

14 $x = 48°$ (vertically opposite)
     $y = 48°$ (F-angles)
     $z = 132°$ (angles on a straight line)

Exercise 26.3

As with all algebra problems, guesswork is not the best approach and should be discouraged. The idea is to write a formal equation to describe the diagram, then solve the equation using the methods practised in Unit 24.

1 $350 + a = 360$; $a = 10°$

2 $100 + 2b = 180$; $b = 40°$

3 $2c + 14 = 3c - 24$; $c = 38°$

4 $270 + 5d = 360$; $d = 18°$

5 $3e + 36 = e + 60$; $e = 12°$
    $5f + 63 = 2f + 90$; $f = 9°$

6 $44 + g = 86 - 2g$; $g = 14°$

7 $2h + 50 = 180$; $h = 65°$

8 $65 + 3j = 95 + j$; $j = 15°$

9 $5k + 20 = 52 + k$; $k = 8°$

10 $m + 36 = 90$; $m = 54°$
     $m + n = 180$; $n = 126°$

Review Exercise 26

1 Rectangle   2 Rhombus

3 Sanjay is wrong – it could be a rhombus.

4 Gita is right.

5

Four lines of symmetry	square
Two lines of symmetry	rectangle rhombus
One line of symmetry	arrowhead kite
No line of symmetry	parallelogram trapezium

6 $a = 30°$ 7 $b = 106°$

8 $c = 111°$ $d = 69°$ $e = 111°$

9 $f = 118°$ $g = 62°$

10 $h = 118°$ 11 $j = 118°$

12 $k = 56°$ 13 $m = 63°$

14 $315 + 3w = 360$; $w = 15°$

15 $114 + 3m = 142 - m$; $m = 7°$

16 $288 + 8y = 360$; $y = 9°$

17 $6z - 30 = 180$; $z = 35°$

18 $a = 136°$

19 $x = 14°$ The quadrilateral is an isosceles trapezium (angles 70°, 110°, 110°, 70°).

20 $y = 10°$, $z = 55°$

Unit 27
Making shapes using *Logo*

Exercise **27.1**

*The aim of the first section is to familiarise the pupils with the basic vocabulary of **Logo**. The use of the repeat command is encouraged, as it allows a reduction in the amount of code needed to draw a regular or symmetrical shape.*

1. A square of side 75 units
2. A rectangle measuring 20 units by 30 units
3. A square of side 60 units
4. A (right-angled isosceles) triangle with sides 50, 50, 71 units
5. An equilateral triangle of side 60 units
6. A regular pentagon of side 50 units
7. A regular hexagon of side 50 units
8. A five-pointed star
9. A parallelogram of sides 20 units and 30 units
10. A staircase with 10 steps, each of 10 units

Exercise **27.2**

*In this section pupils will learn how to write code as a **procedure**; such procedures can then be saved permanently on the computer's hard disk. In MSW **Logo** the instruction 'Save Alan' will save all the currently defined procedures, with their names, under the overall title 'Alan'; there is no need to save them one by one. When next logged on, the instruction 'Load Alan' will then re-load all the procedures previously saved.*

In describing these shapes, precision should be encouraged. 'Draws a rectangle' is too vague.

1. fred: draws a rectangle 50 units by 70 units
2. flag: draws a 30 unit square flag on the end of a 130 unit pole
3. shape: draws an equilateral triangle of side 70 units
4. star: draws a five-pointed star
5. wriggle: draws a 'staircase' but with no right angles
6. letter: draws an elongated letter T
7. octopus: draws a regular octagon of side 30 units
8. roof: draws an isosceles trapezium whose parallel sides are 8 units and 28 units
9. platypus: draws a regular 20-gon (looks very much like a circle)
10. frame: draws a rhombus of side 50 units

Exercise **27.3**

This section gives further practice at writing code. More imaginative pupils might like to design their own shapes on squared paper, then write code to draw them.

1. fd 30 lt 90 fd 60
   repeat 4 [lt 90 fd 10]
2. fd 30 rt 90
   repeat 4 [fd 10 rt 90]
   fd 10
   repeat 4 [fd 10 rt 90]

Level 6 Unit 27

3 lt 90 fd 20 rt 90 fd 30

4 fd 30 lt 90 fd 10 bk 20

5 fd 20 rt 90 fd 10 bk 10 lt 90 fd 20 rt 90 fd 20

6 fd 30 bk 15 rt 90 fd 30 lt 90 fd 15 bk 30

7 fd 30 rt 90 fd 10 rt 90 fd 20 lt 90 fd 10 rt 90 fd 10 rt 90 fd 20

8 fd 20 lt 90 fd 10 rt 90 fd 10 rt 90 fd 30 rt 90 fd 10 rt 90 fd 10 lt 90 fd 20 rt 90 fd 10

9 fd 40 rt 90 fd 30 rt 90 fd 10 rt 90 fd 20 lt 90 fd 10 lt 90 fd 10 rt 90 fd 10 rt 90 fd 10 lt 90 fd 10 rt 90 fd 10

10 repeat 2 [fd 30 rt 90 fd 10 rt 90 fd 10 lt 90 fd 10 lt 90 fd 10 rt 90 fd 10 rt 90]

Exercise 27.4

*This section combines **Logo** skills with an understanding of how to use exterior angles of a regular polygon. The table on page 202 could be constructed as a class activity, using 30 ÷ n to find the exterior angle, then subtracting this from 180° to find the interior angle.*

1 repeat 4 [fd 70 rt 90]

2 repeat 5 [fd 40 rt 72]

3 repeat 6 [fd 50 rt 60]

4 repeat 15 [fd 10 rt 24]

5 repeat 12 [fd 12 rt 30]

6 repeat 18 [fd 25 rt 20]

7 repeat 10 [fd 30 rt 36]

8 repeat 8 [fd 45 rt 45]

9 repeat 9 [fd 40 rt 40]

10 repeat 9 [fd 40 rt 80]

Exercise 27.5

This final section links some of the 2-D geometrical concepts covered in the Unit to 3-D models. Check that vocabulary is used accurately: ***gon (2-D) or ***hedron (3-D).
Polydron kits (or similar) may be useful in some of these questions.

1 2-D shape: dodecagon
3-D shape: dodecahedron, each face is a regular pentagon.

2 (Any two of these three)
Tetrahedron (4 triangles), octahedron (8 triangles) and icosahedron (20 triangles)

3 a) Octahedron
b) Equilateral triangles

4 a) A triangular prism
b) 12 cm

5 Katie has made an octahedron (not necessarily a regular one).

Review Exercise 27

1 A rectangle of sides 100 units and 60 units

2 A parallelogram of sides 100 units and 80 units.

3 A regular decagon of side 40 units.

4 repeat 2 [fd 70 rt 140 fd 70 rt 40]

5 repeat 8 [fd 35 rt 45]

6 repeat 6 [fd 55 rt 60]

7 a) (Computer check)
b) The **cs** will clear away any old drawings which may still be on the screen.
c) The pattern is supposed to represent a cube.

63

Level 6 Unit 27

8. **a)** Usha is trying to represent a square-based pyramid.
   b) The diagram could be improved by adding a dotted line from the top to the remaining corner of the base.

9. **a)** (Computer check)
   b) The star does not join up – because the angle of 62° is too small.
   c) The instruction 'rt 62' should be changed to 'rt 72'.

10* (Computer exercise)

Unit 28
Area and volume

Exercise 28.1

This section gives practice in the use of the standard formula for the area of a triangle. Acute, right-angled and obtuse-angled triangles are all covered, and some of the questions in the exercise deliberately contain extra measurements which are not needed in the calculations.

1. a) 156 cm²   b) 152 cm²
   c) 980 mm²   d) 336 cm²
   e) 33 m²   f) 71.5 cm²
   g) 53.1 cm²   h) 20.9 m²
   i) 18 400 mm²   j) 71 400 mm²
2. 279 cm²
3. 319 cm²
4. 218.5 cm²
5. 150 cm²
6. 178.5 cm²
7. 105.8 cm²

Exercise 28.2

The various results in the table on page 208 should be studied thoroughly before attempting the exercise. Getting the class to make posters about each of the different quadrilaterals can be a worthwhile activity; such posters could feature symmetry properties as well as proofs of the area formulas.

1. Square; 144 cm²
2. Rectangle; 98 cm²
3. Parallelogram; 36 cm²
4. Rhombus; 108 cm²
5. Trapezium; 35 cm²
6. Rhombus; 57.12 cm²
7. Rectangle; 32.76 cm²
8. Parallelogram; 100.75 cm²

Exercise 28.3

The exercise could be extended by using some local examples – such as the area of an irregularly shaped classroom or an oddly-shaped playing field.

1. 184 cm²   2. 1011 cm²   3. 408 cm²
4. 402 cm²   5. 651 cm²   6. 25 cm²

Exercise 28.4

This exercise is a straightforward application of the result for the volume of a cuboid, and should present no major difficulties.

1. 560 cm³   2. 315 cm³   3. 1331 cm³
4. 570.18 cm³   5. 1267.5 cm³   6. 36 in³

Review Exercise 28

1. a) 29.565 cm²   b) 60 cm²
   c) 45.5 cm²   d) 78 cm²
2. a) 182.25 cm²   b) 154 mm²
   c) 432 mm²   d) 165 cm²
   e) 136.5 ft²   f) 3774 mm²
3. 5600 cm³
4. 700 cm³
5.* 29 cm
6.* 19 cm
7.* a) 78 520 cm² (or 7.852 m²)
    b) 777 400 cm³ (or 0.7774 m³)
8.* ABH: 60 m²
   BDIH: 108 m²
   DFJI: 225 m²
   JFG: 82.5 m²
   ACK: 48 m²
   CKLE: 127.5 m²
   ELG: 76.5 m²
   Total: 727.5 m²

Unit 29
The circle: area and circumference

Exercise 29.1

Pupils should check carefully whether they are working with the radius or the diameter. Avoid writing answers to the full calculator display (10 figures) – sensible rounding should be encouraged.

1	50.3 cm	2	113 cm
3	31.4 km	4	62.8 cm
5	88.0 mm	6	75.4 mm
7	44.0 km	8	59.7 m
9	37.7 cm	10	6.28 cm
11	9.111 m	12	9.425 cm
13	134.5 mm	14	25.76 cm
15	94.25 cm	16	196.3 mm
17	2.907 km	18	76.97 km
19	7885 mm	20	3.167 km

Exercise 29.2

As with the previous section, pupils should check whether the radius or diameter has been given. Answers should be rounded off, and have appropriate units of area.

1	201 cm^2	2	1020 cm^2
3	78.5 km^2	4	314 cm^2
5	616 mm^2	6	452 mm^2
7	154 km^2	8	284 m^2
9	113 cm^2	10	3.14 cm^2
11	6.605 m^2	12	7.069 cm^2
13	1439 mm^2	14	52.81 cm^2
15	706.9 cm^2	16	3068 mm^2
17	0.6723 km^2	18	471.4 km^2

19 4 948 000 mm^2 or 4.948 m^2
20 0.7980 km^2

Exercise 29.3

The examples should be studied carefully before attempting the exercise. When the area is given the radius is found by dividing by π and then square rooting; check that pupils are doing these two processes in the right order.

1	5.57 mm	2	3.18 in
3	3.34 mm	4	1.20 m
5	37.4 mm	6	16.6 cm
7	1.75 m	8	2.76 cm
9	0.574 mm	10	1350 km

Review Exercise 29

1 119 cm
2 661 cm^2
3 151 cm
4 3 800 000 mm^2 or 3.80 m^2
5 Circumference 169.6 cm, area 2290 cm^2
6 Circumference 290 mm, area 6800 mm^2
7 17.6 cm
8 377 mm
9 9.77 cm
10 15.8 m
11* a) 0.374 m
    b) 0.600 m
    c) Richard is right
12* a) 2160 people
    b) 239 m
13* a) 3.90 m
    b) 47.8 m^2
14* a) 28.3 cm^2 b) 36 cm^2
    c) 21%

Level 6 Unit 29

15* a) 580 million miles
   b) 940 million kilometres
16* a) 1.78 m
   b) 9.98 m^2
   c) 250 penguins
17* The blue disc is larger (red radius 6.21 cm, blue radius 8.28 cm)
18* a) 201 cm
   b) 600 000 cm
   c) 2985 times
19* a) Circumference 37.7 cm, area 113 cm^2
   b) Circumference 75.4 cm, area 452 cm^2
   c) '…it should have twice the circumference and *four times* the area…'
20* 11.1 m

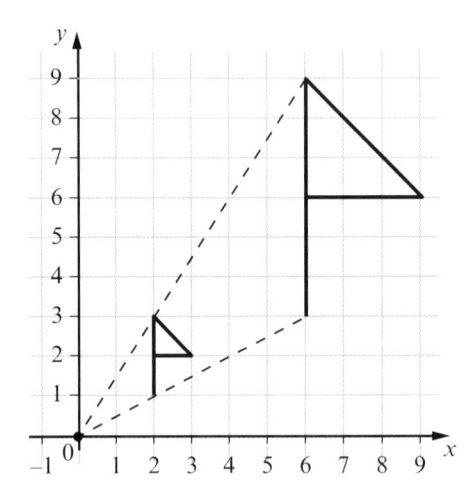

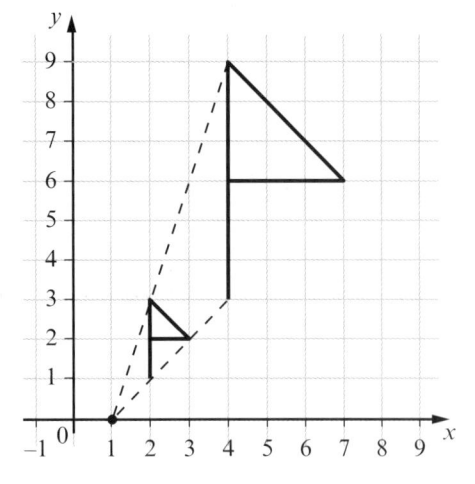

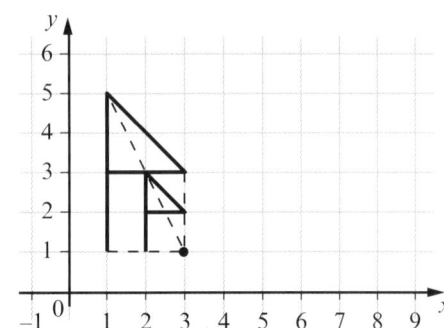

Unit 30
Enlargement and reflection

Exercise **30.1**

Careful ray tracing is to be encouraged in this introductory section. Pupils who find it difficult to construct accurate drawings might benefit from the use of photocopied grids and diagrams, prepared by teacher in advance.

More able pupils might do these problems by a kind of vector approach (e.g. 'go two across and one up, two across and one up again, etc.') although their concept of vector is not formally developed at this stage.

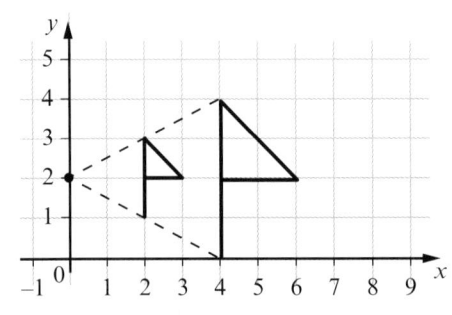

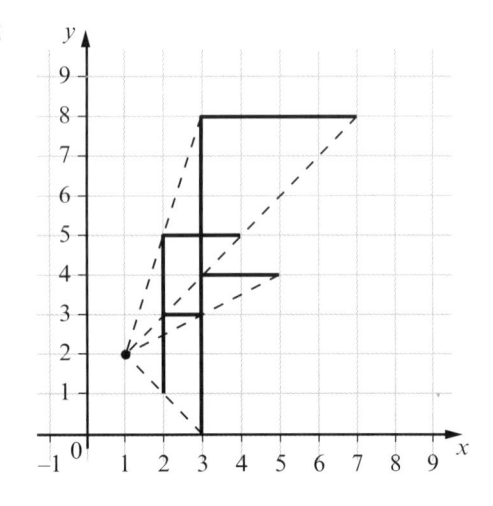

6

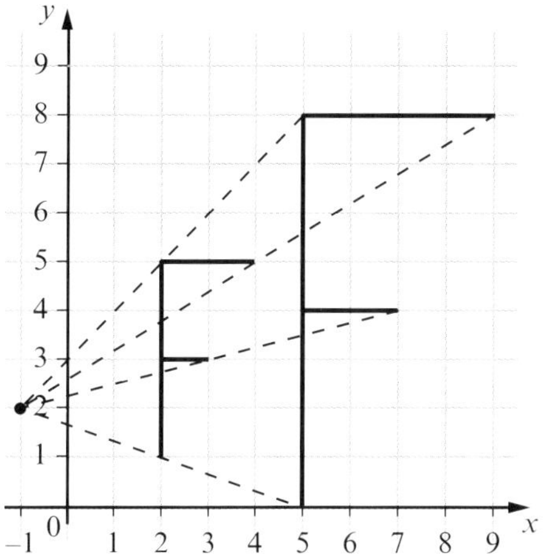

9

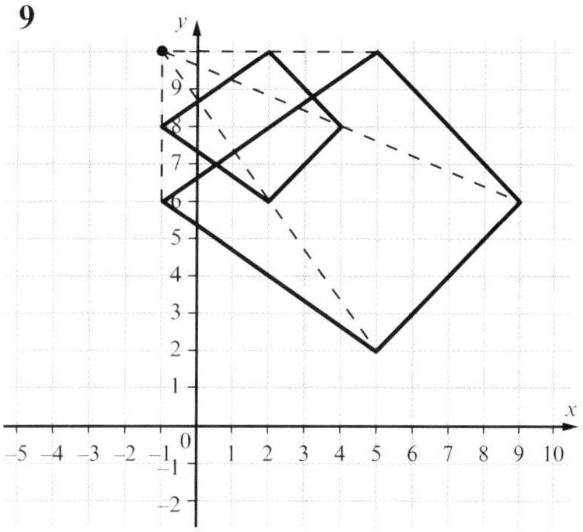

7

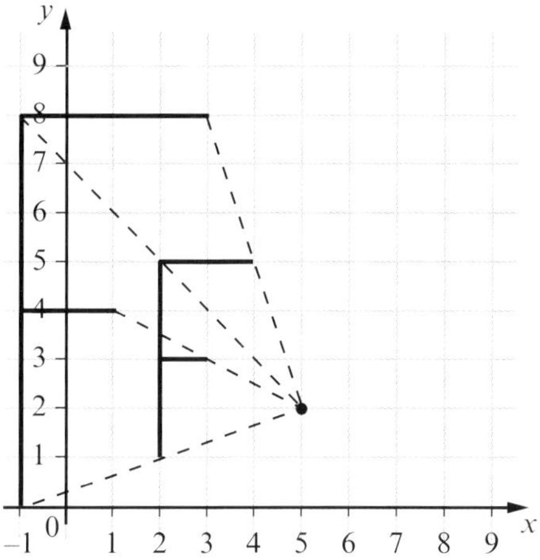

10

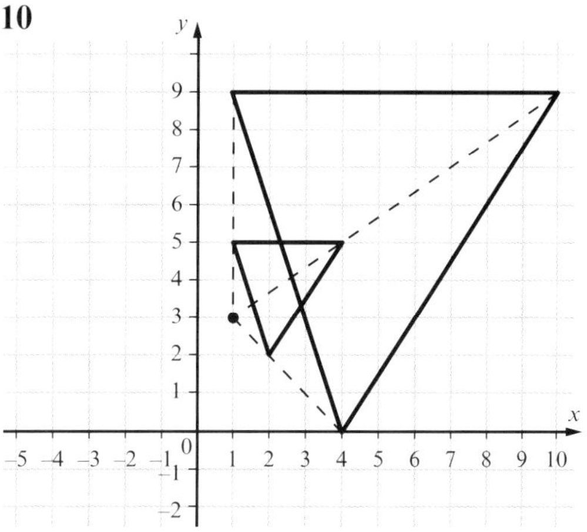

8

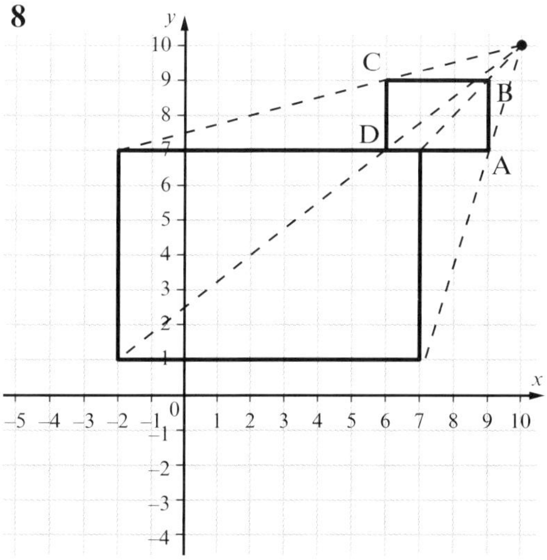

Exercise 30.2

Once again, careful ray tracing is to be encouraged. Corresponding key points on the object and image must be identified before any rays are constructed.

1 Centre (–1, 1), scale factor 4

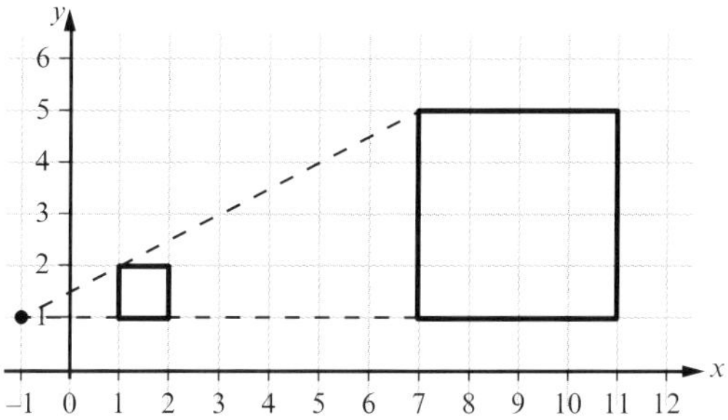

Level 6 Unit 30

2 Centre (11, 4), scale factor 2

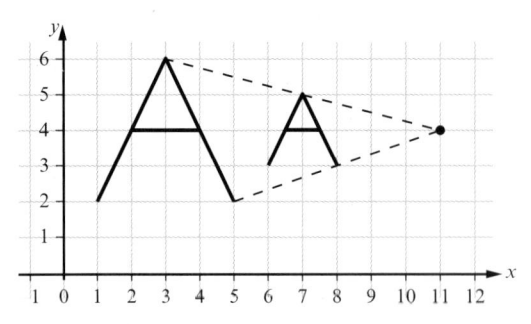

3 Centre (11, 2), scale factor 2

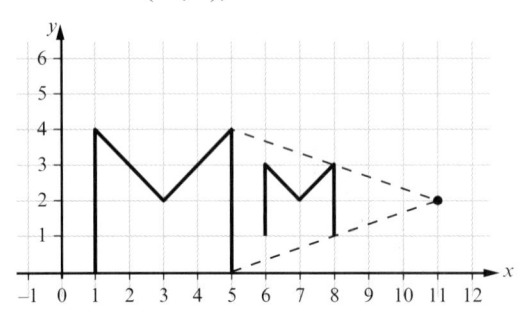

4 Centre (–1, 0), scale factor 3

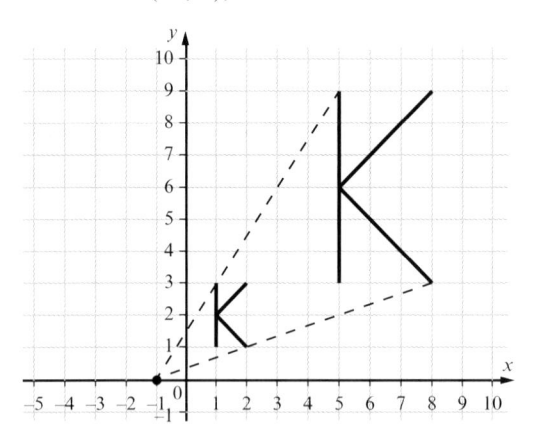

5 Centre (0, –1), scale factor 2

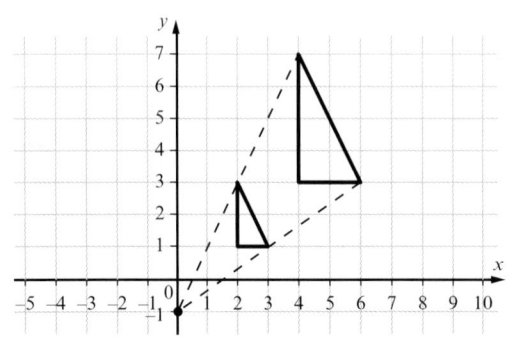

Exercise 30.3

This short section introduces the idea of two transformations. Consider extending this by looking at what happens when the same two transformations are done in the opposite order – is the overall result necessarily the same/different?
The whole topic can be rounded off nicely by making some posters for the classroom.

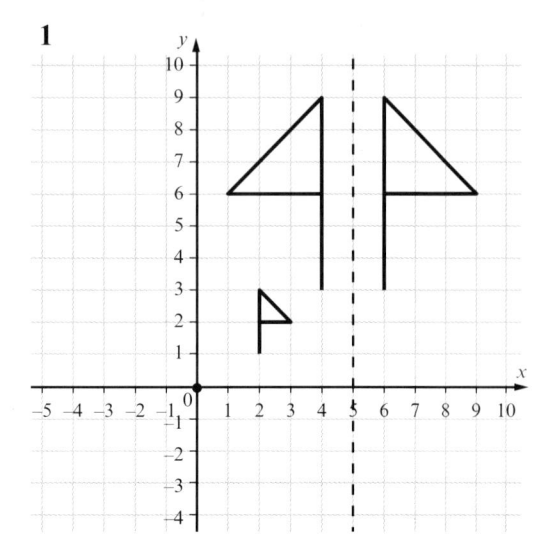

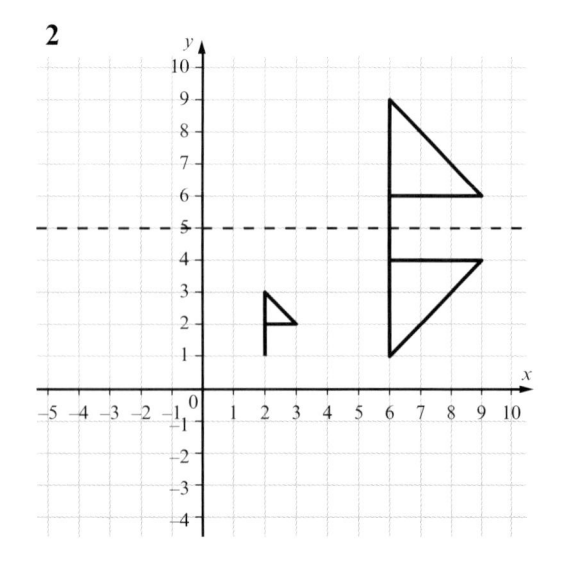

1

2

Level 6 Unit 30

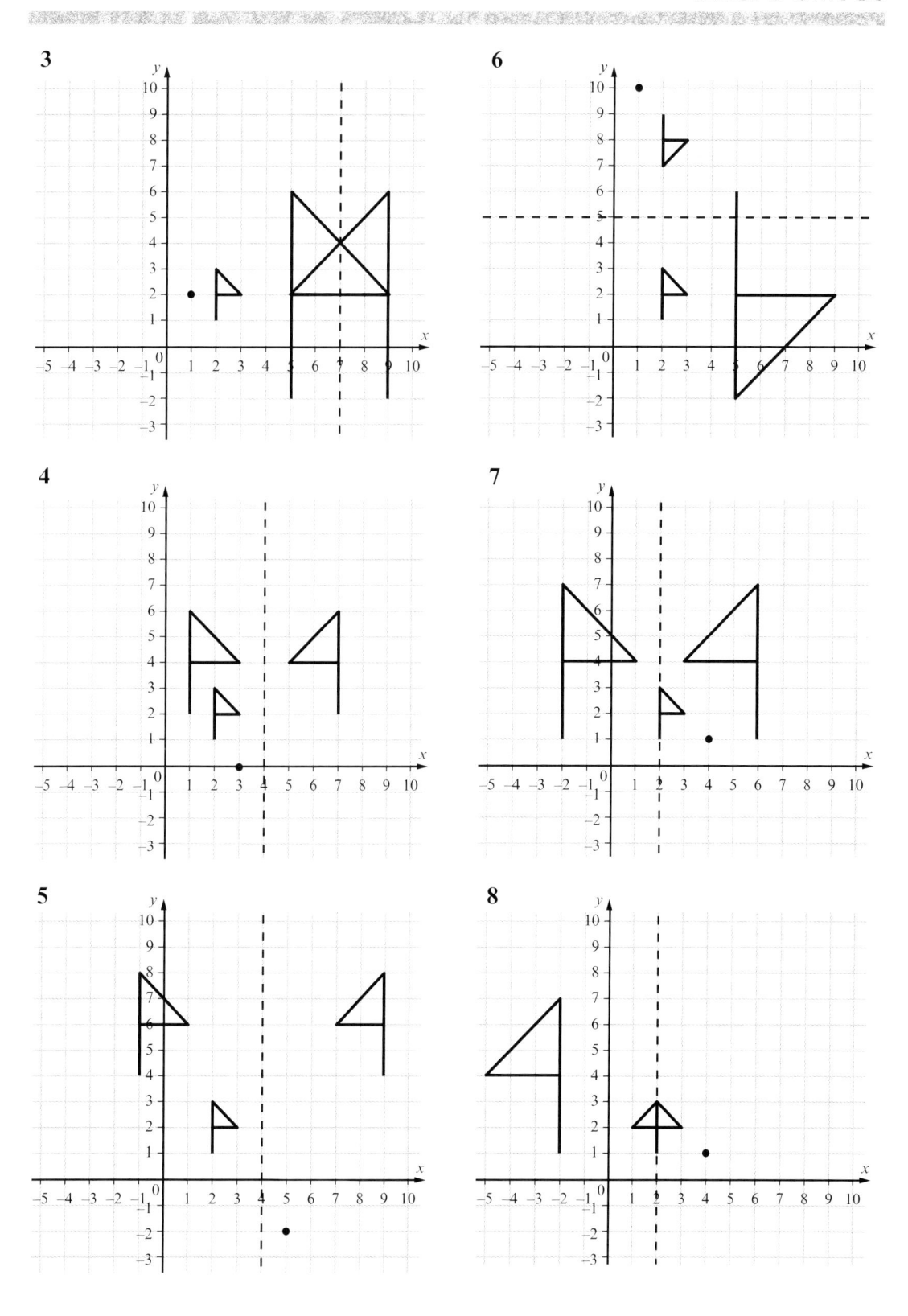

3

4

5

6

7

8

Review Exercise 30

1

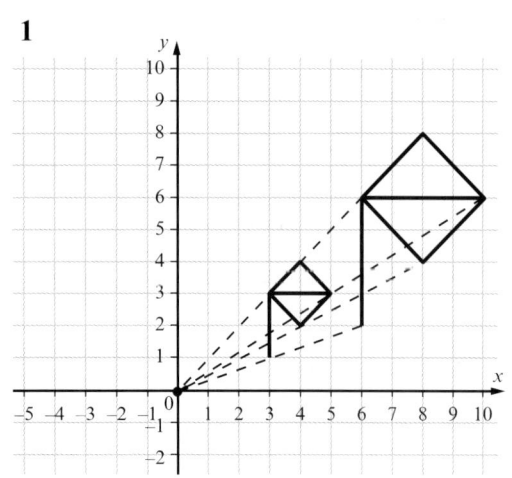

2

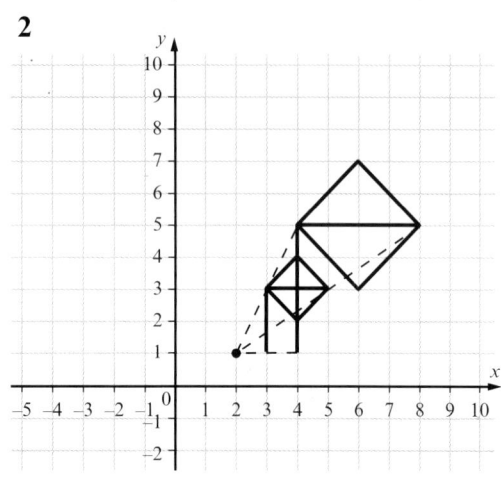

3

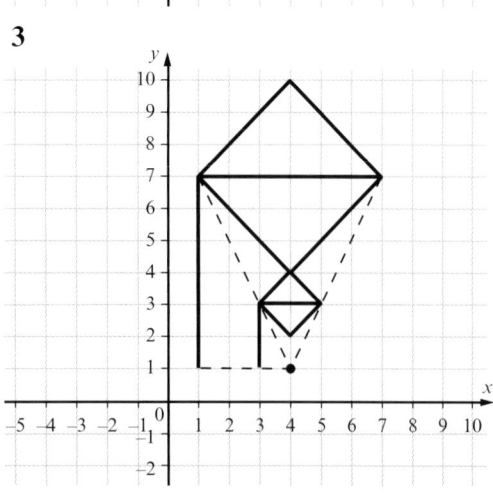

4

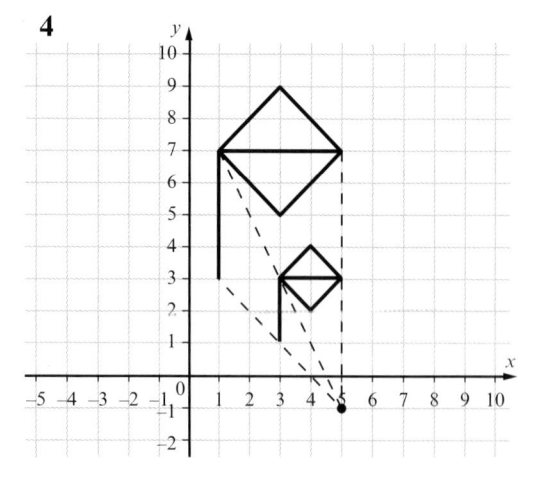

5

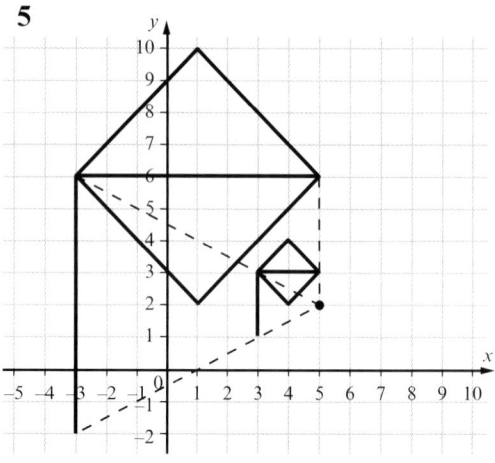

6

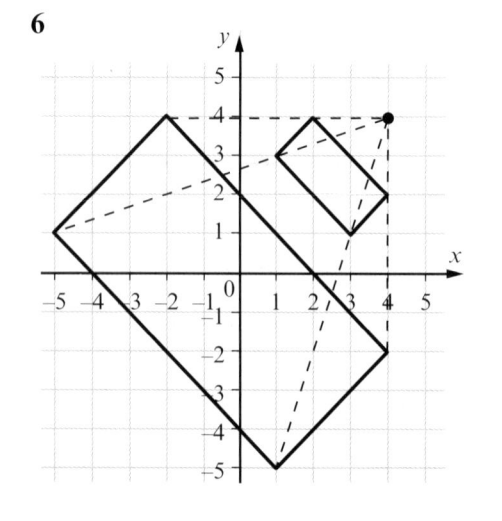

Level 6 Unit 30

7

8 a)

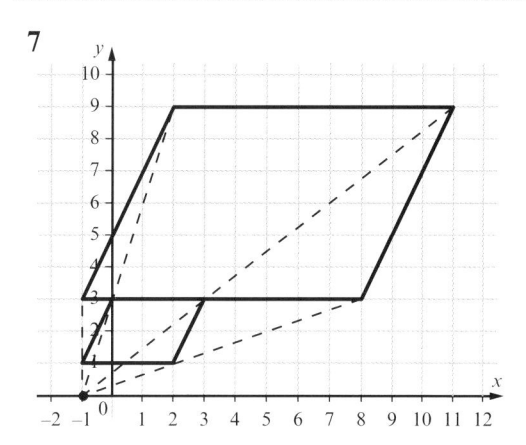

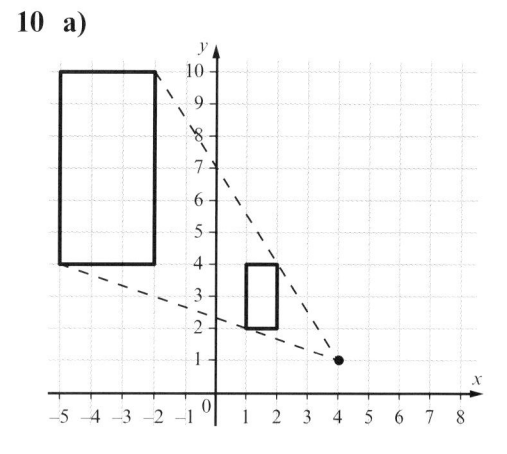

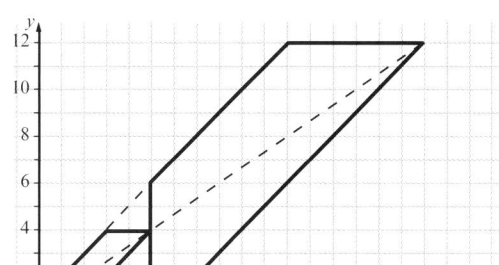

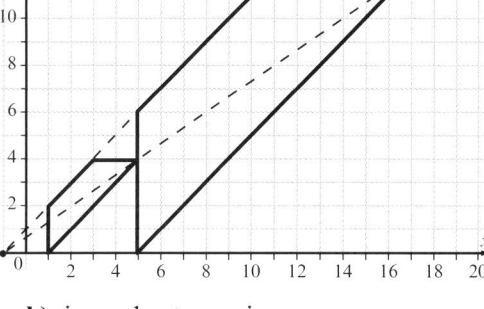

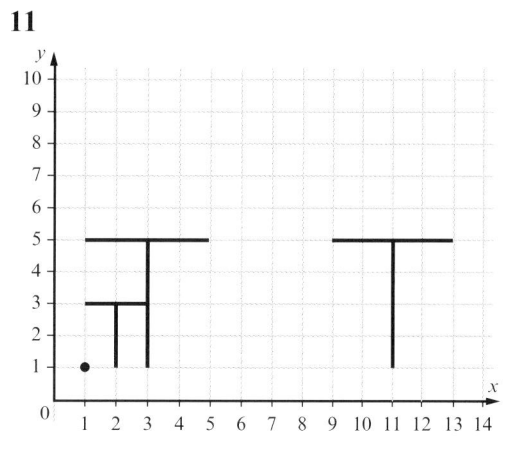

b) isosceles trapezium

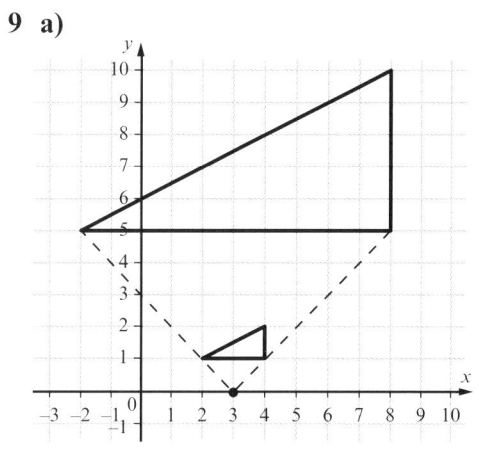

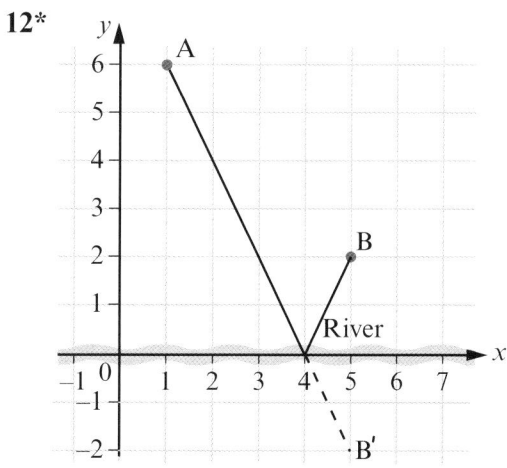

9 a)

b) centre (3, 0), scale factor 5

10 a)

b) centre (4, 1), scale factor 3

11

12*

73

Level 6 Unit 30

13*

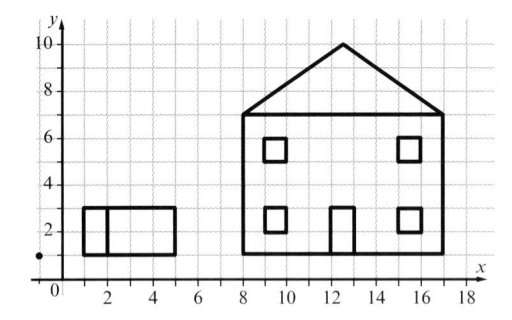

14* Anna is right.

15*

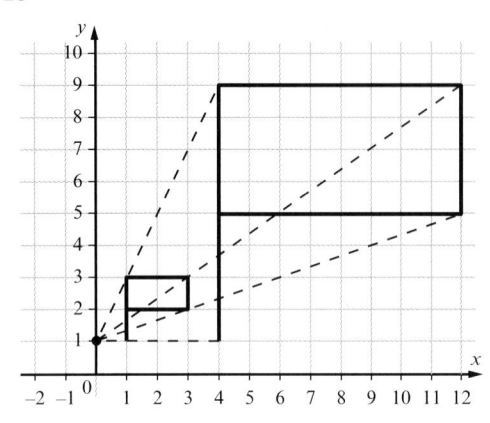

Unit 31
Frequency diagrams and pie charts

Exercise 31.1

Some of these answers are not as simple as they may seem! Question 2, the length of a CD track in minutes, is continuous provided decimals are used as well; if the track length is written down to the nearest minute then we are making a discrete approximation to a continuous variable. Some pupils will feel that the answer to question 9, the amount of money in a bank account, is continuous, as units of £1 are subdivided using decimals. The key point here is that there is still a unit, albeit £0.01, and the amount of money must go up or down in multiples of this. A nice illustration is a money box – you use counting, not measurement, to find the amount.

1. Discrete
2. Continuous
3. Continuous
4. Discrete
5. Continuous
6. Discrete
7. Continuous
8. Discrete
9. Discrete
10. Continuous

Exercise 31.2

Pupils should be shown examples of other notation, such as 15–20, 20–25 and even 15– , 20– etc. The notation used throughout this Unit is superior, since it enables the treatment of endpoints to be described accurately.

1. a)

Mass (g)	Frequency
$100 \leq x < 110$	1
$110 \leq x < 120$	0
$120 \leq x < 130$	5
$130 \leq x < 140$	11
$140 \leq x < 150$	5
$150 \leq x < 160$	3

b) 32%

2. a)

Height (cm)	Frequency
$100 \leq x < 110$	4
$110 \leq x < 120$	9
$120 \leq x < 130$	12
$130 \leq x < 140$	3
$140 \leq x < 150$	2

b) 25 children

3. a)

Age (years)	Frequency
$0 \leq x < 5$	3
$5 \leq x < 10$	0
$10 \leq x < 15$	17
$15 \leq x < 20$	14

b) The storm probably took place two years ago.

Level 6 Unit 31

Exercise 31.3

Histograms and frequency polygons are constructed using exactly the same principles; if the mid-points of the tops of the bars on a histogram are joined up the result is a frequency polygon.

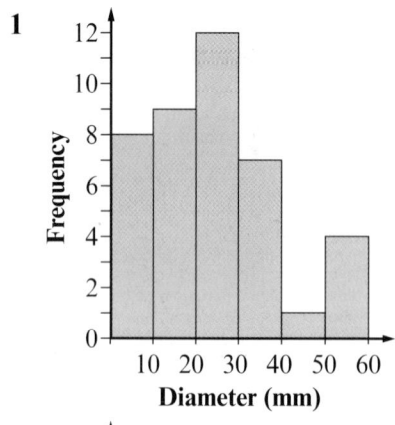

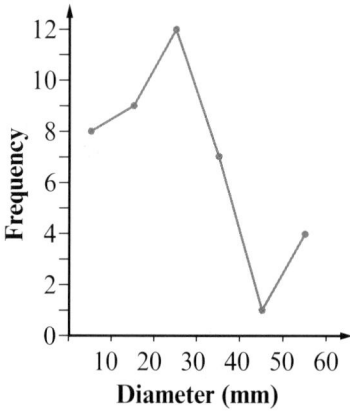

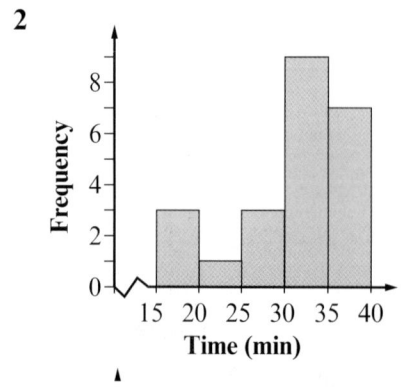

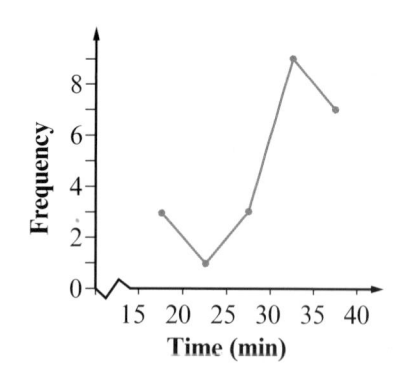

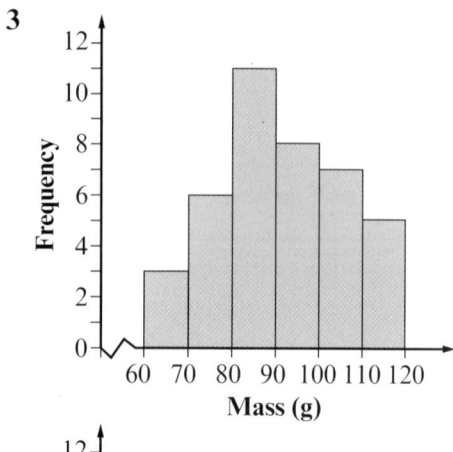

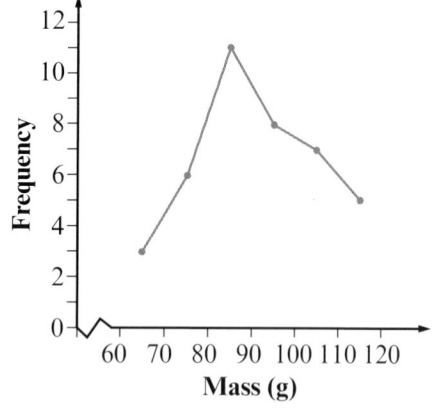

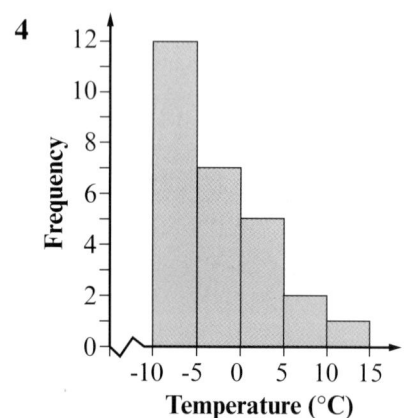

1.

2.

3.

4.

Level 6 Unit 31

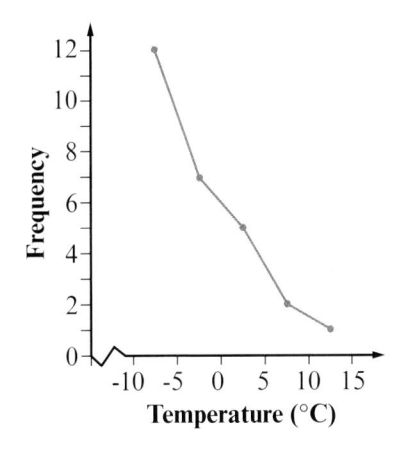

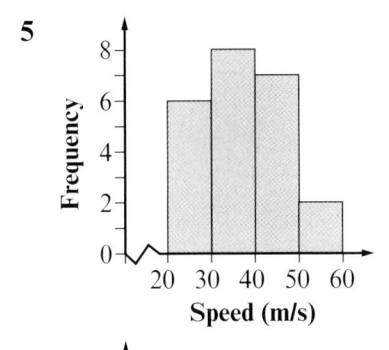

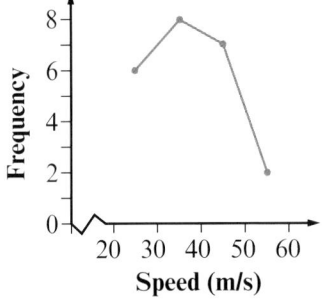

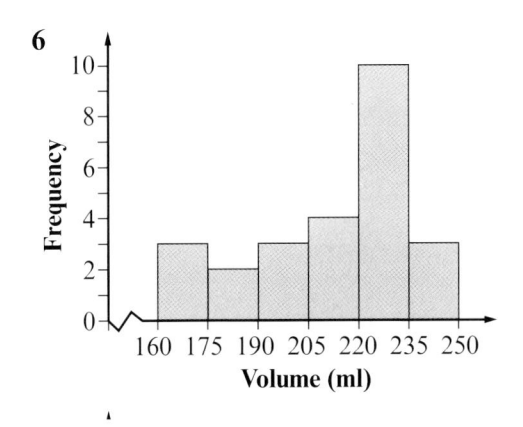

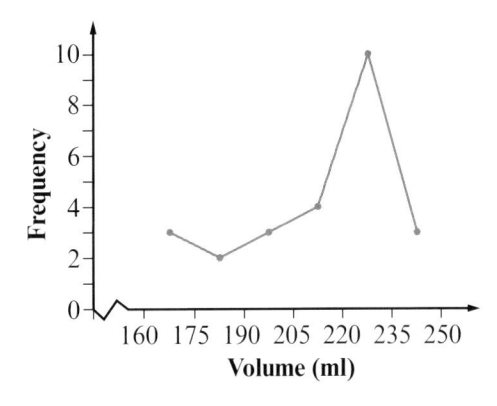

Exercise 31.4

In this section pie chart sectors are scaled up by 360° ÷ (total) so that the various angles add up, in theory, to 360°. In practice, rounded values may well add up to 361° or 359° – this may be an unavoidable consequence of the process of rounding.

1

Country	Great Britain	France	Germany	Other
Angle	172°	82°	41°	65°

2

Country	Dairy	Cash crops	Woodland	Feed
Angle	154°	75°	41°	89°

3 Angles: puppies 133°, kittens 114°, ponies 69°, rabbits 44°

4 Angles: sunny 197°, overcast 105°, wet 58°

Review Exercise 31

1 Discrete
2 Continuous
3 Discrete
4 Discrete
5 Continuous
6 Continuous

Level 6 Unit 31

7 a)

Time	Tally	Frequency
$0 \leq t < 1$	I	1
$1 \leq t < 2$		0
$2 \leq t < 3$	ⅢⅡ I	6
$3 \leq t < 4$	ⅢⅡ IIII	9
$4 \leq t < 5$	II	2
$5 \leq t < 6$	I	1
$6 \leq t < 7$	I	1

b) $\frac{13}{20}$ or 0.65

8 a)

Body length	Tally	Frequency
$140 \leq l < 150$	II	2
$150 \leq l < 160$	III	3
$160 \leq l < 170$	ⅢⅡ	5
$170 \leq l < 180$	ⅢⅡ IIII	9
$180 \leq l < 190$	I	1
$190 \leq l < 200$	III	3
$200 \leq l < 210$	I	1

b)

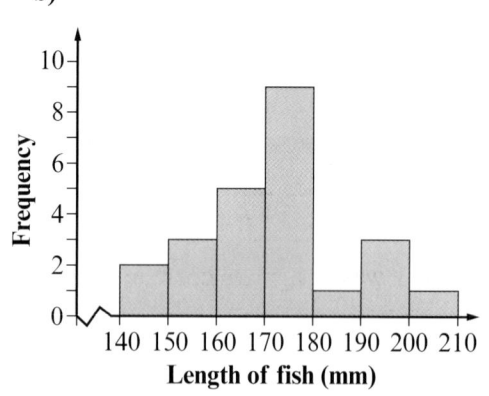

c) 75%

9 Angles: sparrows 165°, starlings 134°, blackbirds 51°, robins 10°

10* a) Angles: BBC 153°, ITV 126°, Channel 4 54°, BBC 2 27°

b) The data suggests that Alice lives in a part of the country where Channel 5 was not available in 1997.

11* a) A frequency polygon is better, because the data is continuous numerical data, not categorical data.

b)

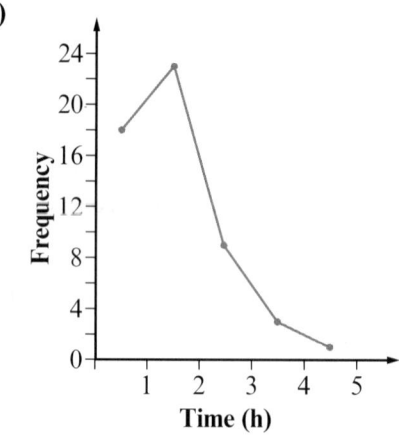

12* a) 23 children

b) 125°

Unit 32
Scatter diagrams and other graphs

Exercise 32.1

In this section pupils will describe whether there is evidence of positive or negative correlation. In addition they should say whether the correlation is strong or weak – some subjective judgements may be made in this respect.

1 Strong positive correlation

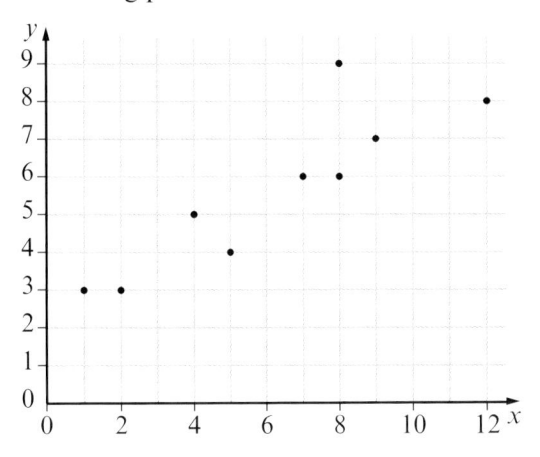

2 No correlation

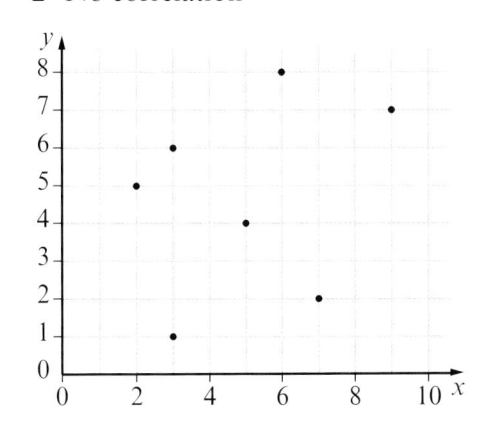

3 Weak positive correlation

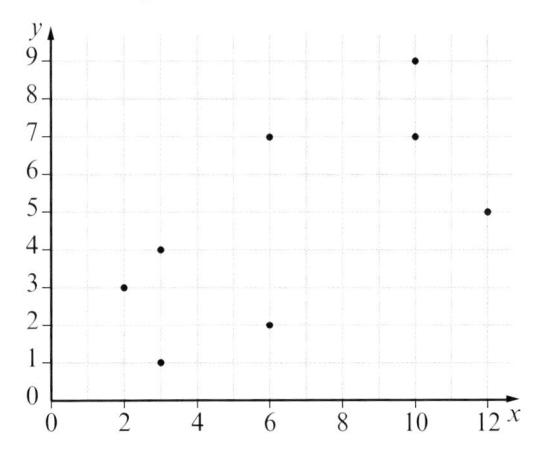

4 Strong negative correlation

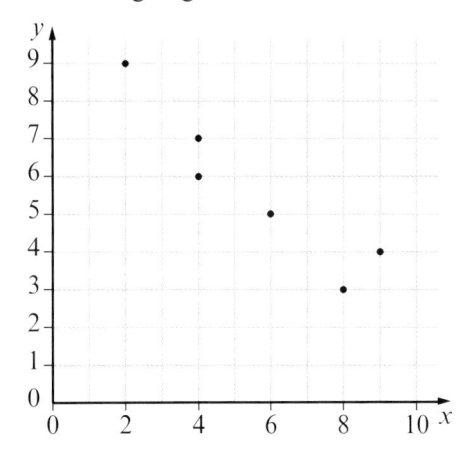

5 Very weak negative correlation (or no correlation at all).

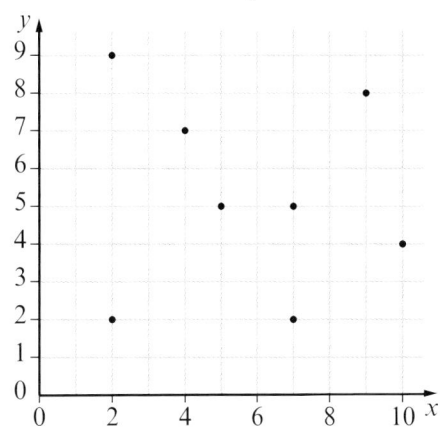

Level 6 Unit 32

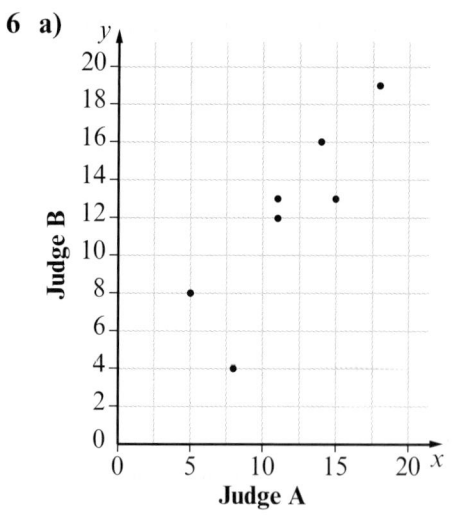

6 a)

graph: Judge B vs Judge A scatter plot

b) There is strong positive correlation between the two sets of marks.

7 a) Plant A probably died.
b)

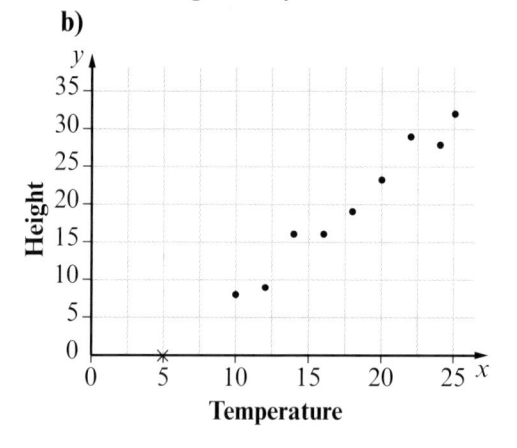

graph: Height vs Temperature scatter plot

c) The height and temperature show strong positive correlation.

Exercise 32.2

The answers to these questions are only approximate, as they are read from a graph. A conversion graph is a useful device for obtaining a quick, rough answer, though nowadays a spreadsheet offers an equally quick and far more accurate alternative.

1 b) About 70 km
   c) About 88 miles

2 b) About 11 kg
   c) About 66 pounds

3 a) $165
   c) About $140
   d) About £40

4 a) 182 litres
   c) About 114 litres
   d) About 8.8 gallons

5 a) 20.2 hectares
   c) 37 acres
   d) 6 hectares

Exercise 32.3

This section contains a few questions on other types of graph. An interesting class project is for pupils to collect different types of graph from newspapers and magazines etc. for a classroom display. Newspapers often rely on pie charts rather too much, but on the other hand some unusual graphic designs can also be found.

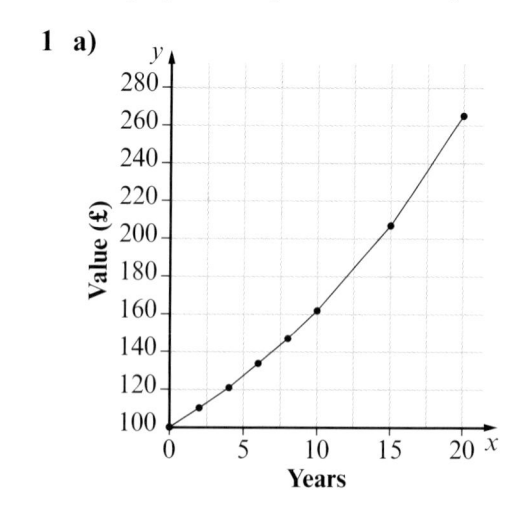

1 a)

graph: Value (£) vs Years curve

b) About £178

80

2 a)

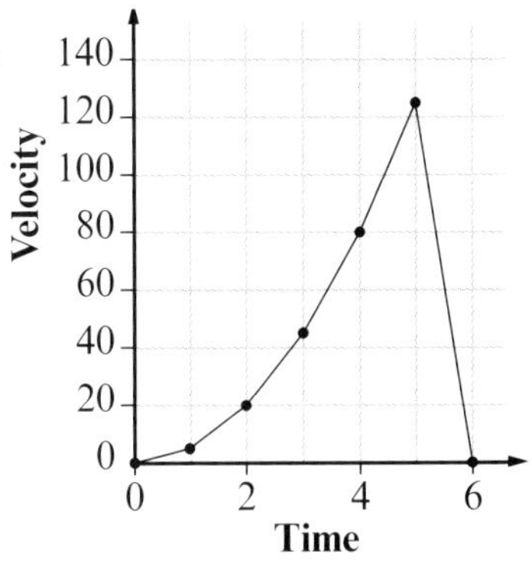

b) 101 m/s **c)** 2.8 seconds

d) It lands between 5 and 6 seconds after being dropped.

3 a)

Greenview School roll

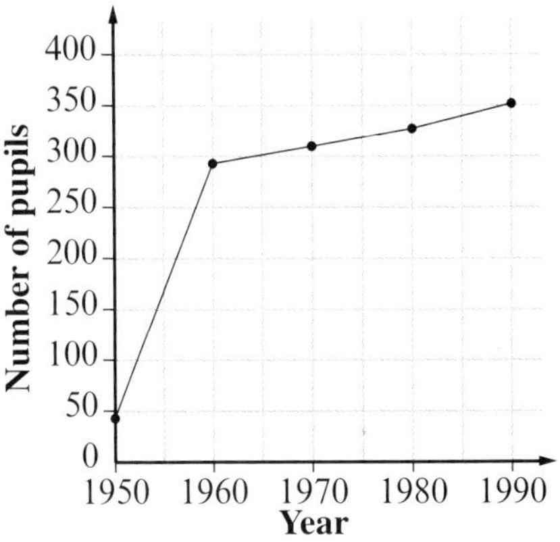

b) 1964 **c)** 1985

Review Exercise 32

1 a)

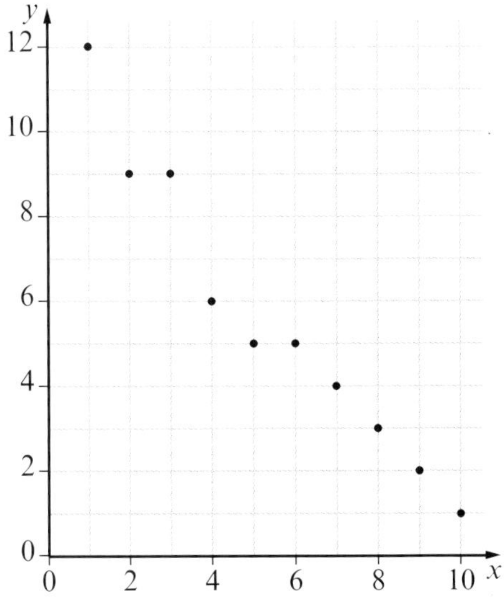

b) x and y show strong negative correlation.

2 a)

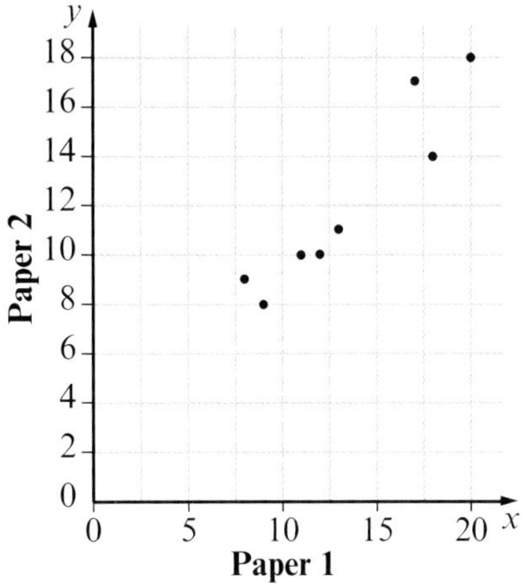

b) The two marks show strong positive correlation.

c) Joe's marks do not fit the rest of the data. Perhaps he got some help with Paper 2!

3 a)

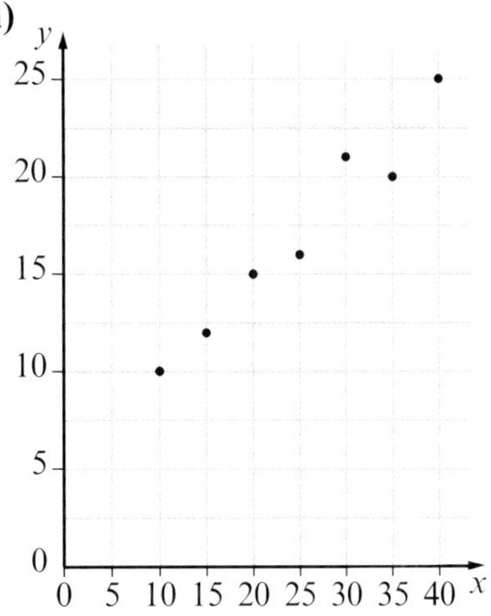

b) x and y show strong positive correlation.

Level 6 Unit 32

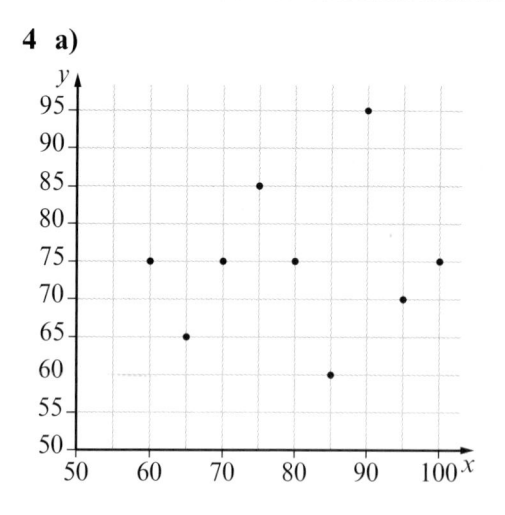

4 a)

[scatter graph with y-axis from 50 to 95, x-axis from 50 to 100]

b) The verbal and numerical scores do not appear to be correlated.

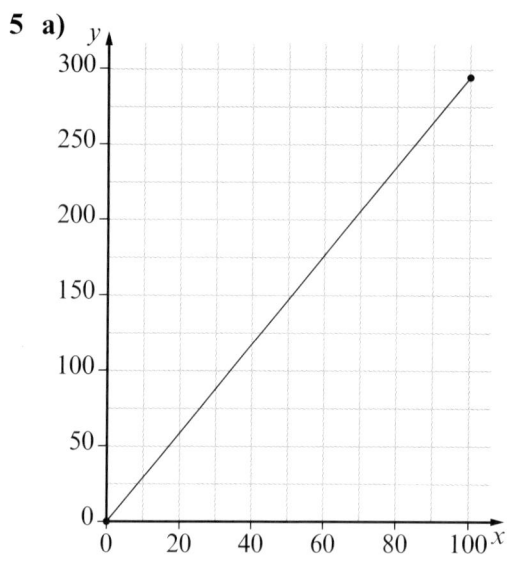

5 a)

[line graph, y-axis from 0 to 300, x-axis from 0 to 100]

b) About £69   **c)** About £37

6 a) 32.6 light years

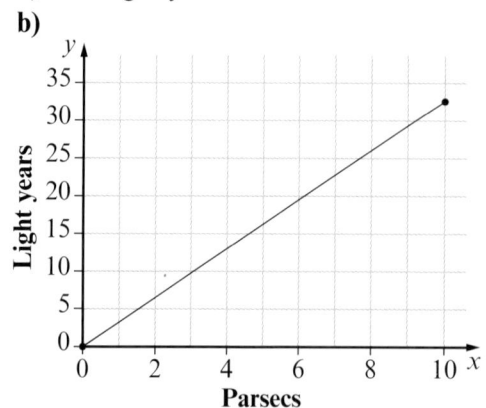

b)

[line graph, Light years (y) from 0 to 35, Parsecs (x) from 0 to 10]

c) About 28 light years

d) About 2.6 parsecs

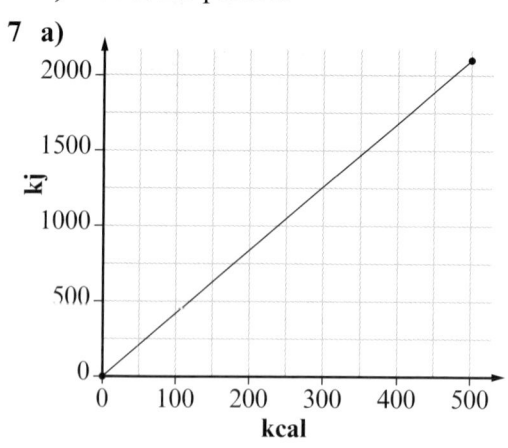

7 a)

[line graph, kJ from 0 to 2000, kcal from 0 to 500]

b) About 210 kcal per 100 g

c) About 1670 kJ

8* a) and b)

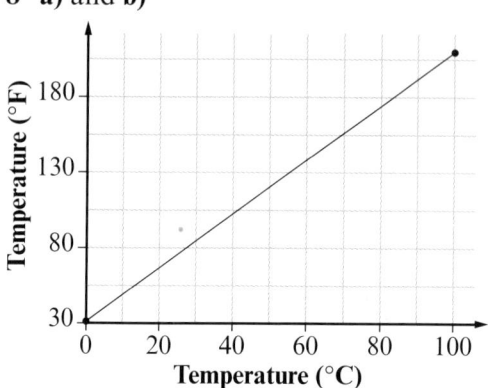

[line graph, Temperature (°F) from 30 to 180, Temperature (°C) from 0 to 100]

c) 86° F, 82°C

d) y is not directly proportional to x; the graph is a straight line but does not pass through the origin.

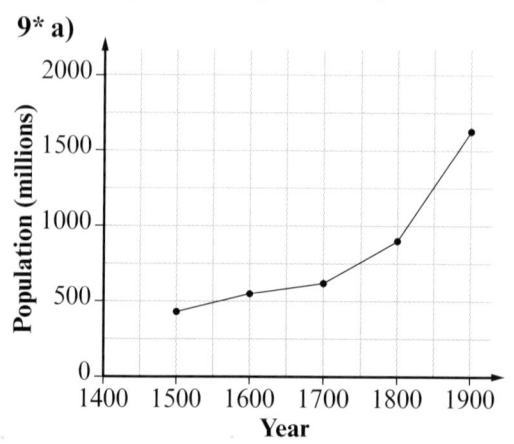

9* a)

[line graph, Population (millions) from 0 to 2000, Year from 1400 to 1900]

82

b) i) about 480 million;
ii) about 750 million

c) The graph is rising very steeply beyond 1900; it is difficult to tell how much steeper it is becoming.

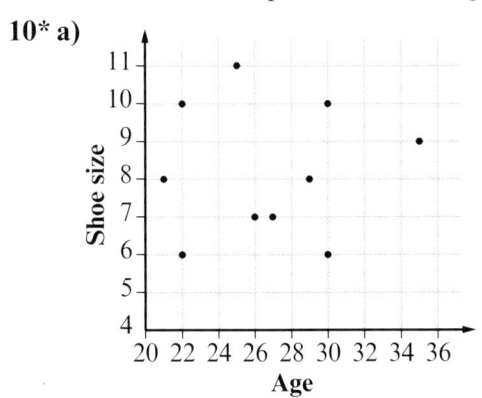

10* a)

[Scatter graph of Shoe size (vertical, 4–11) against Age (horizontal, 20–36)]

b) There is no evidence of correlation between age and shoe size.

c) Naomi's data is based on young children – younger children tend to have smaller feet than older children, so she sees strong positive correlation. Andrei's data is based on adults who have finished growing, so their shoe sizes are more scattered, giving no correlation.

Unit 33
Probability

Exercise **33.1**

In this section sample space diagrams are drawn to give a picture of all the equally likely outcomes. The required probability can then be found by counting. Attempts to solve the problems without making a drawing should, at this stage, be discouraged.

1. a) $\frac{1}{2}$ b) $\frac{5}{12}$ c) $\frac{1}{9}$
2. $\frac{3}{16}$
3. $\frac{1}{9}$
4. a) $\frac{1}{4}$ b) $\frac{1}{4}$ c) $\frac{1}{2}$
5. $\frac{1}{5}$ The most likely score is 4 or 5 or 6, all of which are equally likely.
6. a) $\frac{1}{6}$ b) $\frac{1}{4}$
7. a) $\frac{1}{5}$ b) $\frac{7}{15}$
8. a) $\frac{1}{16}$ b) $\frac{1}{4}$
9. $\frac{2}{9}$
10. a) $\frac{1}{9}$ b) $\frac{1}{18}$ c) $\frac{1}{4}$
    d) $\frac{1}{6}$

Exercise **33.2**

As with sample spaces, the purpose of a tree diagram is to help visualise the problem, so diagram-free solutions should be discouraged. The points about multiplying along the branches but adding different endpoints are well worth stressing; some find it helpful to use the rule that 'and means multiply; or means add.' Like all such rules, it should be used with care!

1. 0.36
2. a) 0.0625   b) 0.375
3. 0.4475
4. 0.384
5. a) 0.14   b) 0.06   c) 0.62
6. a) 0.25   b) 0.42   c) 0.834
7. 0.422
8. a) 0.05   b) 0.171
9. a) $\frac{1}{5}$ = 0.2   b) 0.008   c) 0.384
10. a) 0.25   b) 0.3   c) 0.04

Review Exercise **33**

1. a) 0.25   b) 0.0156
2. a) $\frac{1}{3}$ b) $\frac{1}{9}$ c) $\frac{4}{9}$
3. a) $\frac{1}{12}$ b) $\frac{1}{6}$ c) $\frac{11}{36}$
4. a) $\frac{2}{9}$ b) $\frac{7}{9}$ c) $\frac{1}{3}$
5. a) 0.7
   b)

```
           0.3 ─── V
      0.3 ─ V ⟨
   ⟨           0.7 ─── C
      0.7 ─ C ⟨
           0.3 ─── V
               0.7 ─── C
```

   c) 0.21   d) 0.42

6. a)

	1	1	1	1	1	6
1	2	2	2	2	2	7
1	2	2	2	2	2	7
1	2	2	2	2	2	7
1	2	2	2	2	2	7
1	2	2	2	2	2	7
6	7	7	7	7	7	12

   b) $\frac{5}{18}$ c) $\frac{13}{18}$

Level 6 Unit 33

7* a)

First coin	Second coin	Third coin
H	H	T
H	T	H
T	H	H
T	T	H
T	H	T
H	T	T
T	T	T
H	H	H

  b) $\frac{1}{8}$ **c)** $\frac{3}{8}$

8* a) 0.729   **b)** 0.001   **c)** 0.243

9* a) 0.6   **b)** 8

10* a) When he chooses the second sock there are only five in the drawer, not six.

  b) $\frac{2}{6} \times \frac{1}{5} = \frac{1}{15}$

Level 6 Review

Exercise 1
1. 3.1416
2. 76.0
3. 450.3
4. 76.2
5. 6.01, 6.03, 6.099, 6.18, 6.3
6. 17, 20
7. 15, 20
8. £90
9. 80%
10. 25%
11. 32.5%
12. 70%
13. 0.62
14. 1.06
15. 0.96
16. 5:3
17. 2, 5, 8
18. 1, 2, 5
19. −4
20. 9

Exercise 2
1. £15
2. 100 francs
3. £27.50
4. 84p
5. £13.50 per square metre
6. 24 girls
7. 81 cm²
8. 60 cm²
9. A rhombus
10. One
11. Four
12. 48 000
13. £3.75
14. 80°
15. Hexagon
16. Octagon
17. Octahedron
18. 25 cm²
19. 20
20. 7

Exercise 3
1. $u_{n+1} = u_n + 4$ and $u_1 = 3$
2. $u_n = 2^{n-1} + 1$
3. 62%
4. 35%
5. 70%
6. 6%
7. 9:7:5
8. 4
9. 5
10. 7

11. 80 cm²
12. 120 cm²
13. $\frac{7}{12}$
14. 0.5, Boris is the better player.
15. It doesn't have to be a kite – it depends on the lengths of the sides, which are not given. Gary is wrong to say it must be a kite.
16. Lucy is right.
17. A square of side 80 units.
18. A parallelogram with sides 80 and 50 units.
19. A regular pentagon of side 90 units.
20. A five-pointed star (pentagram).

Exercise 4
1. 8.5
2. 1.38
3.

x	−3	−2	−1	0	1	2	3
x^2	9	4	1	0	1	4	9
$3x$	−9	−6	−3	0	3	6	9
−1	−1	−1	−1	−1	−1	−1	−1
y	−1	−3	−3	−1	3	9	17

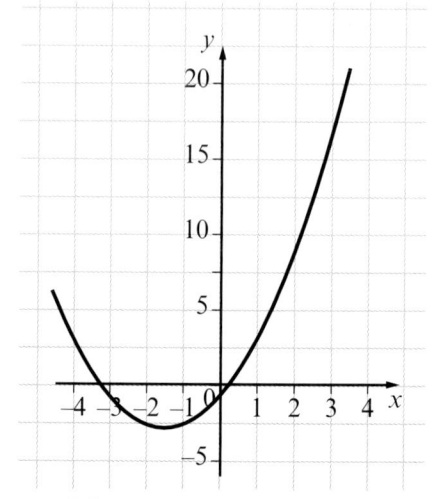

$x = 0.3$

Level 6 Review

4 a) (−1, 2)   **b)** ×3

5 a) 9 eggs, 225 g of caster sugar, 75 g of cocoa powder.
  b) The metric/imperial conversions are only approximate.

6 $11x + 30 = 360$
   $x = 30$
   The angles are 35°, 75°, 100° and 150°

7 $a = 49°$, $b = 131°$, $c = 59°$, $d = 121°$, $e = 121°$, $f = 59°$

8 50.3 cm   **9** 1385 cm^2

10 28.6 m   **11** 7.6 cm

12 a) A   **b)** D   **c)** B

13 10 sides

14 360° is not exactly divisible by 26°.

15 a) 36 boys   **b)** 38 girls
  c)

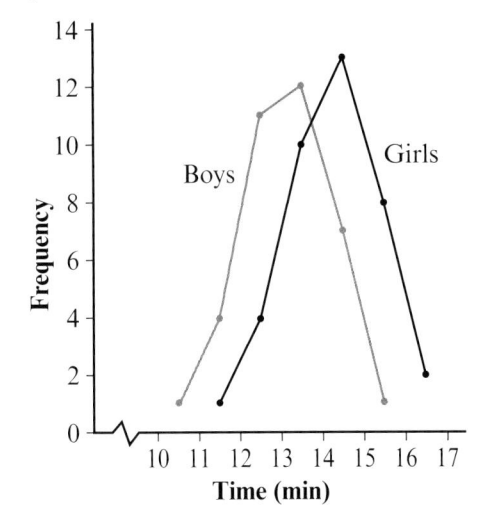

[Frequency polygon comparing Boys and Girls times (min) from 10 to 17, with Boys peaking at 12 min (frequency 12) and Girls peaking at 14 min (frequency 13).]

  d) The girls are taking about 1 minute longer, on average.

87